Shashi Kapoor
The Householder, the Star

Shashi Kapoor
The Householder, the Star

ASEEM CHHABRA

With a Foreword by Karan Johar

RUPA

Published by
Rupa Publications India Pvt. Ltd 2016
7/16, Ansari Road, Daryaganj
New Delhi 110002

Sales centres:
Allahabad Bengaluru Chennai
Hyderabad Jaipur Kathmandu
Kolkata Mumbai

ISBN: 978-81-291-3970-2

First impression 2016

10 9 8 7 6 5 4 3 2 1

The moral right of the author has been asserted.

Typeset by SÜRYA, New Delhi
Printed at Replika Press Pvt. Ltd., India

*To my mother, who shared her love for films and
movie stars with me*

*And to Ishan—here's sharing my love for films and
movie stars with you*

Contents

Foreword

It was the 1960s. A dashingly handsome, dimpled hero with abnormally good hair had arrived on the scene. In lush green hill stations, he'd look lovingly at his heroines. And for that split second, time would stop, as would the hearts of members of the audience.

The hero was Shashi Kapoor. And he was every bit the romantic heart-throb—from his mannerisms and his looks to that *je ne sais quoi* that makes hearts flutter and women fall in love. Shashi Kapoor was the quintessential Prince Charming.

Then came the late 1970s and the early 1980s, when the idea of a hero changed. He became a middle-class, rage-fuelled man who communicated with his fists, rather than with words. Affectionate glances were replaced by angry tears. The audience went wild, seeking graphic violence and scenes that went crash-boom-bang on the screen. The Prince Charming of the preceding decade seemed almost buried.

And yet, Shashi Kapoor miraculously survived. With his fascinating screen personality and great acting skills, he continued leaving a mark as the voice of reason and morality. He became an antidote to the 'revenge or nothing' phase that Bollywood seemed to be passing through. The characters he essayed reminded the audience that amidst the sound and fury, the blood and violence, there was still value in quiet graciousness and gentleness; there was merit in abiding by what-is-right, as opposed to reacting reflexively to what's-right-now. Shashi Kapoor was now the 'moral hero'.

Shashi Kapoor has been a stalwart of the film industry for years, and was one of the first actors to consistently act in international cinema. Yet, throughout, he had remained a humble man, known to treat every member of the crew as his own. He is also one of the few to unfailingly return to his roots—theatre. His establishment of Prithvi and even his role in the international movie *Shakespeare Wallah* have been tributes to everything that theatre had given him in his youth—his finesse, his command over his craft and, of course, his wife. Shashi Kapoor is the 'ultimate gentleman'.

Somewhere, in the hullaballoo of the over-the-top 1980s phase of Indian cinema, we forgot what a great actor and human being Shashi Kapoor was and continues to be. I have the greatest love and respect for him—not just for his contribution to our industry, but also for the person he is: always kind, always engaging and always generous.

Today, I am honoured to write about a man who never gave up on his craft, but nurtured it as a producer, a theatre veteran and even as a producer who picked interesting, offbeat subjects to back. Shashiji has the love and respect of a generation that grew up watching him light up the screen every single time. And indeed, anyone who is to discover him today will undoubtedly feel the same way.

To me, and to a great many people, he will always be the gentleman, the moral hero, a Prince Charming.

He will always be Shashi Kapoor.

Karan Johar
Bombay, 2016

Author's Note

Normally, as a journalist, when I refer to someone, I use the full name the first time, but retain the last name (or surname) in later references. In this book, though, the practice would have caused some bewilderment since I talk about many Kapoors—Shashi Kapoor, Raj Kapoor, Shammi Kapoor, Sanjna Kapoor, Kunal Kapoor and even Rishi Kapoor. So I chose to use full names the first time, and the first name thereafter.

This decision did not make things any easier. In the Indian film industry, older actors and filmmakers are often addressed with respect and a 'ji' or a 'da' (among Bengalis) is added to the first name. So, Yash Chopra is usually addressed as Yashji, and Bimal Roy is mostly called Bimalda. Shyam Benegal, in fact, is called Shyam Babu by everyone in the film industry. It is honorific and a tradition. But there are some in the industry who have reminded me to drop the 'ji', even though they are older than me—so, Rishi Kapoor must be called Rishi, and Aparna Sen, Aparna.

Therefore, for the sake of consistency, I have had to abandon tradition and protocol. I mean no disrespect to anyone, but I must follow a thread of logic. While it might seem strange to some readers, in second usage situations in each section I generally refer to people—young or senior—just by the first name. That is the case with Amitabh, Shyam, Shashi and even Satyajit. I hope I will be forgiven for making this judgement call.

I'd like to add that in those cases where there are no citations, the quotes have been extracted from one-on-one interviews.

Finally, while Poona was officially designated as Pune in 1978, Bombay as Mumbai in 1995, Madras as Chennai in 1996, and Calcutta as Kolkata in 2001, in this book, the older spelling has been retained for consistency.

INTRODUCTION

On 5 January 1985—a day after I got married in Delhi—I stepped into the lobby of the Taj Mansingh Hotel with my new bride. A short while earlier, we had had a slight argument—our first in a marriage that lasted fifteen years. As we walked side by side, a strange kind of discomfort lingered between us.

And then, as we looked straight ahead, I saw Shashi Kapoor standing by the reception, elegantly dressed in a dark suit and a tie. My wife had a big crush on Shashi—something I was aware of. I remember watching a VHS tape of *Bombay Talkie*,[1] that scintillating film directed by James Ivory, with her parents and her, back when we were still courting. My wife shocked her mother as she gave a long sigh when Shashi (as Vikram) kissed Jennifer Kendal Kapoor (as Lucia) in a shot in a hotel room. (Incidentally, this was the only time Shashi and Jennifer, real-life husband and wife, played on-screen lovers.)

'Look, there's Shashi Kapoor!' I whispered to my wife, pointing towards the reception. Suddenly, her demeanour changed; she was no longer upset, but rapt.

Soon, a young woman sauntered up to the actor and loudly said, 'Hello, Shashi, remember me?' The whole lobby echoed with her voice. 'No,' the actor responded as he looked at her.

I imagine the lady thought that hers was a perfectly good line

with which to approach a movie star. I am also certain that Shashi
had never met this woman—it is a well-known fact that the actor,
for the longest time, had a photographic memory for the most
fleeting of acquaintances.

That was where the evening should have ended—with the
disenchanted lady slinking away, and my wife being happier for
the sighting—our first fight coming to an abrupt close, thanks to
the enigmatic Shashi.

And yet, the evening returned in the most unexpected manner
in early 2015, when I was researching for this book. I happened to
interview filmmaker Ramesh Sharma who directed Shashi in *New
Delhi Times*.[2] Ramesh told me that the shooting of the film had
been delayed for a number of reasons and, finally, some parts of
the movie were shot in Delhi in late 1984 and early 1985. Despite
the film's tight budget, Shashi was the only member of the cast to
have stayed at the Taj Mansingh. When I told Ramesh that I had
seen Shashi in the hotel's lobby, he immediately confirmed what I
had now concluded: 'That's when I was making the film!'

I felt as though a certain circle had been completed. A story I
had told friends at multiple dinner parties—about my then-wife
and me running into Shashi—now had an added layer, another
meaning.

When I look back, I see that Shashi had found a way of
sneaking into my childhood recollections, too. Decades earlier, in
the summer of 1964, I had been a little kid on vacation in Srinagar
with my parents. I have vague memories of staying in a houseboat;
of being turned away while on a shikara ride on the Dal Lake
because a 'movie shoot' was in session; and of hearing that the film
was *Jab Jab Phool Khile*[3]—Shashi and Nanda were acting in it.

I do not think at that age—I was less than ten years old—I had
caught any film with Shashi or Nanda. But I think I knew who
they were. And I remember feeling rather thrilled that I was on
the same lake as two movie stars; soon after, I know I was

overwhelmed by crushing disappointment—I had missed seeing
the stars and the shoot.

Later, when I was in school in Delhi, a group of my class
friends and I wrote letters to Shashi and Sharmila Tagore. Someone
in my school had managed to get their addresses in Bombay and
we all decided to pen what must been childish fan mails, doubtless
read by the stars' managers. I remember receiving two postcards—
one from Shashi and another from Sharmila, perhaps in envelopes.
They had been coloured—black-and-white photographs touched
up with ink. Shashi's lips were a bright pink. It made him look
rather pretty, a tad bit effeminate. But none of that concerned me
then. What mattered was the personal connection I had established
with a terribly good-looking and very likeable movie star.

Little did I know in school that three decades later I'd spot
Shashi at the Prithvi Café in Juhu, Bombay, talking to a couple of
people. This was long before this book had been planned. Since I
refuse to stalk celebrities—and approach them only if my job as a
film journalist demands it—I did not disturb him that evening.
The scene, though, remains etched in my mind—an older Shashi,
seated on a chair like so many others, refusing to draw any attention
to himself.

By the time this book was planned, Shashi's health was on the
decline. And so, I could not talk to him. His daughter, Sanjna
Kapoor, tells me that he has dementia, while his nephew, Rishi
Kapoor, says that he cannot hear too well and has trouble
recognizing people.

*

As I pieced together interviews for this book, I realized that many
people had forgotten Shashi Kapoor. I would hear young women
say that only their mothers or grandmothers had crushes on him.
And my cousin's kids, now in their teens, came to learn of Shashi
for the first time when I explained to them, in terms they could

understand, 'He is Rishi Kapoor's uncle, Ranbir Kapoor's grand
uncle.' A few of those in their thirties remembered Shashi from
Yash Chopra's *Deewaar*[4]—though even this iconic film, as a
British-Pakistani friend informed me, was recalled more for
Amitabh Bachchan than his striking co-star. How odd, I thought;
yes, Amitabh (as Vijay) did have a more flamboyant role in *Deewaar*,
but that performance would have been lost without the balance
and calm that Shashi (as Ravi) offered.

Fortunately, soon after I started working on this biography,
Shashi was honoured with the Dadasaheb Phalke Award for his
contribution to Indian cinema. It was a much deserved accolade
and it reinstated him in public memory. It was also long overdue.
Filmmaker Shyam Benegal says as much to me: 'Now that I
consider it, I got the Dadasaheb Phalke Award in 2005. Shashi
got it ten years later. He should have received it earlier, and well
before I did.'

But Shashi is not one to bear a grudge. His oldest child, Kunal
Kapoor, reveals: 'When told about being conferred the highly
prestigious Dadasaheb Phalke Award for his immense contribution
to films, all (my father) did was smile and nod.'[5] Later, Kunal
adds, 'His reaction to the news of the Dadasaheb Phalke Award
was: "Who me?" and then he chuckled.'

*

Who is the real Shashi Kapoor?

He was definitely India's first international star—long before
the Priyanka Chopras and Irrfan Khans made their mark in
Hollywood.

He was also, by all counts, the most handsome Hindi film
actor of that period—a fact corroborated by almost everyone I've
spoken to, from Sharmila Tagore to James Ivory. 'He was just *so*
good looking,' Shabana Azmi, his co-actor in several films, tells
me. 'In fact, I sincerely believe that his good looks went against

him. Because the first impression was that of a strikingly attractive man, people would forget what a fine actor he was!'

Then, there is Shashi, the producer, who backed some of the best independent movies in India in the 1970s and 1980s. He encouraged filmmakers to take risks, even if it meant that this would eventually drive him to bankruptcy. Kunal Kapoor says that his father refused to forget the debt he owed an industry that gave him his privileged position as a star; he wanted to support the world that he was part of. 'He believed in this,' Kunal tells me. 'He would actually complain about other actors who would become stars, make money, secure a good life, but then, never contribute to the place that nurtured them.'

There's Shashi, the theatre enthusiast, who used to love the immediacy of the stage, and invested all his money in that renowned institution in Bombay, Prithvi. His fondness for theatre was inherited from his father, Prithviraj Kapoor—who worked in films to keep his first love, Prithvi Theatres, operational—and honed by his father-in-law and wife, Jennifer Kendal Kapoor. Shashi and Jennifer built Prithvi on the same plot of land in Juhu that Prithviraj had leased a few decades earlier to create a permanent home for his Prithvi Theatres. 'This is what we grew up with, what my father taught me and what his father taught him,' Sanjna Kapoor, Shashi's daughter, tells me.

Through Sanjna and Kunal Kapoor, we get glimpses of Shashi, the family man, who loved his wife dearly and did all he could to support his household, even if it meant acting in a few rather terrible (but well-paying) movies. To the surprise of almost everyone, Shashi could easily transition between art-house and American productions, and mainstream Hindi films. In 1982, he acted in the hit comedy *Namak Halaal*[6] with Amitabh Bachchan. The next year, Shashi appeared in James Ivory's critically acclaimed *Heat and Dust*,[7] which was in competition at the Cannes Film Festival. Earlier, in 1978, he produced and played the lead in the

National Award-winning *Junoon*.[8] Months later, he appeared in
Subhash Ghai's *Gautam Govinda*.[9] Once Shashi embraced a role,
he accepted the terms of that project.

In this respect, Shashi's career actually paralleled that of Sharmila
Tagore. She, too, transitioned smoothly between films directed by
Satyajit Ray (*Apur Sansar*,[10] *Devi*,[11] *Nayak*,[12] *Seemabaddha*[13]) and
those by Shakti Samanta (*An Evening in Paris*,[14] *Aradhana*,[15]
Amar Prem[16]) and Yash Chopra (*Waqt*,[17] *Daag*[18]). Both Shashi
and Sharmila understood the place of each type of cinema, and
gladly worked through different systems and sensibilities.

Finally, there's Shashi, the idealist, who could always see people
with an equal eye; it's something that Pamela Chopra, wife of the
late Yash Chopra, confirms. 'Shashi on the sets would treat each
person, from the producer down to the smallest actor, uniformly.'
Sharmila, his frequent co-star and friend, adds: 'Not just fellow
actors and producers—if you talk to technicians, you will learn
that Shashi had their support. He would shake hands with them,
say "*Mera naam Shashi Kapoor hai*" ("My name is Shashi Kapoor")
and have tea in their company.' Neetu Singh Kapoor, who is
married to Rishi Kapoor, and starred opposite Shashi in *Deewaar*,
among other films, echoes this sentiment: 'I remember what a
gentleman he was on the sets of that film. He would talk to the
make-up man, his kid, with everybody. So human and *so* down to
earth.'

Ramesh Talwar, who was the chief assistant director for a
number of Yash Chopra films, remembers this aspect of Shashi's
personality shining through while shooting *Kabhi Kabhie*[19] in
Kashmir. He says, 'Shashi would often host donga (Kashmiri
boat) parties. He would hire two boats and people were free to sit
wherever they liked. The crew often felt awkward mingling with
the stars, but Shashi encouraged people to float from one boat to
the next.'

Kunal says that such inclusiveness was a function of his dad's upbringing. 'My father strongly believed in *his* father's romantic, socialistic ideas. He never stepped on people's toes. He never axed an actor. He never played politics to get a role. He was not competitive. In fact, he was a victim and lost many roles in films because other actors strode in.'

Not surprisingly, Shashi developed a reputation as an eminently likeable star. In fact, when I speak to Sharmila, I realize that this impression cut across not only the industry's pecking order, but also age groups! Sharmila tells me: 'Shashi and I were in Jaipur for *Paap Aur Punya*.[20] My son, Saif (Ali Khan, now an actor), who was just two years old, was with me, as were Shashi's wife and kids. The Kapoors would take my son around, and Shashi, I imagine, spent time playing with him—because soon, Saif grew quite attached to "Shashi Uncle". One day, Shashi happened to be shooting a scene where a villain put a noose around his neck, while he yanked at the rope and struggled quite desperately. Suddenly, the villain, who was in complete command of the scene, screamed! Unknown to him, Saif had crawled up and bitten him on the leg! You see, Saif thought that his Shashi Uncle was being beaten up, was in huge danger, and nobody was helping him. He had to act! Shashi Uncle was really his favourite.' What's rare is that the star didn't even have to work hard to get into the little boy's good books. 'Shashi was just a very likeable guy,' Sharmila smiles. 'It came to him naturally. He didn't need to pretend.'

For me, though, of all the personas Shashi displays, the grandest is undoubtedly that of the star—a hero who has always charmed the movie fan in me. I still love watching the young, handsome Shashi—as Raja, the shikarawallah, smiling and being rather naïve while Rita (Nanda) dances in a white silk gown to 'Yeh Sama, Sama Hai Ye Pyar Ka'[21] in *Jab Jab Phool Khile*; or as the dashing Pyarelal who tries to woo Seema (Asha Parekh), singing 'Ni Sultana Re'[22] in *Pyar Ka Mausam*.[23] And who can forget the actor's despair as he sings in Kishore Kumar's haunting voice,

'Kaise Kahen Hum Pyar Ne Humko',[24] when his character, Captain Ajay Kapoor, is duped into marrying the wrong twin (both roles played by Raakhee) in *Sharmeelee*?[25] Even Kishore Kumar sounds like he is weeping–singing that song!

In writing this book, I want readers to discover each of these Shashi Kapoors, but especially through his films. There are the early works of the 1960s and 1970s that established him as a star of Hindi cinema, and then, several key films that will form a part of his legacy. There is no actual count of how many movies he acted in. Many—such as *Sammy and Rosie Get Laid*,[26] *Jinnah*[27] and *Side Streets*[28]—never got theatre releases in India, and a few—such as *Siddhartha*[29] and *Heat and Dust*—have been forgotten today. But the landmark films—*Deewaar*, *Kabhi Kabhie*, *Junoon*, *Kalyug*,[30] and even one of his first works, *Dharmputra*[31]—are still part of Hindi film history, and are definitely worth revisiting, if only to find the terrific, nuanced actor lurking inside that very attractive man!

Notes

1. 1970, *Bombay Talkie*, dir. James Ivory, prod. Ismail Merchant, starring Shashi Kapoor, Jennifer Kendal, Zia Mohyeddin.
2. 1986, *New Delhi Times*, dir. Ramesh Sharma, prod. P.K. Tiwari, starring Shashi Kapoor, Sharmila Tagore, Om Puri.
3. 1965, *Jab Jab Phool Khile*, dir. Suraj Prakash, prod. Chetan K., starring Shashi Kapoor, Nanda, Agha.
4. 1975, *Deewaar*, dir. Yash Chopra, prod. Gulshan Rai, starring Amitabh Bachchan, Shashi Kapoor, Neetu Singh, Parveen Babi.
5. Quoted in media interviews soon after the award ceremony; also in Surekha Kadapa-Bose, 'Shashi Kapoor: Restricted but Unrelenting', *Dawn*, 9 April 2015.
6. 1982, *Namak Halaal*, dir. Prakash Mehra, prod. Satyendra Pal, starring Amitabh Bachchan, Shashi Kapoor, Smita Patil, Waheeda Rehman, Parveen Babi.
7. 1983, *Heat and Dust*, dir. James Ivory, prod. Ismail Merchant, starring Julie Christie, Greta Scacchi, Shashi Kapoor.

8. 1978, *Junoon*, dir. Shyam Benegal, prod. Shashi Kapoor, starring Shashi Kapoor, Shabana Azmi, Jennifer Kendal.
9. 1979, *Gautam Govinda*, dir. Subhash Ghai, prod. Shyam Sunder Shivdasani, starring Shashi Kapoor, Shatrughan Sinha, Moushumi Chatterjee.
10. 1959, *Apur Sansar*, dir. Satyajit Ray, prod. Satyajit Ray, starring Soumitra Chatterjee, Sharmila Tagore, Alok Chakravarty.
11. 1960, *Devi*, dir. Satyajit Ray, prod. Satyajit Ray, starring Soumitra Chatterjee, Sharmila Tagore, Chhabi Biswas.
12. 1966, *Nayak*, dir. Satyajit Ray, prod. R.D. Bansal, Sharankumari Bansal, starring Uttam Kumar, Sharmila Tagore, Bireswar Sen.
13. 1971, *Seemabaddha*, dir. Satyajit Ray, prod. Bharat Shumsher Jung Bahadur Rana, starring Barun Chanda, Harindranath Chattopadhyay, Sharmila Tagore.
14. 1967, *An Evening in Paris*, dir. Shakti Samanta, prod. Shakti Samanta, starring Shammi Kapoor, Sharmila Tagore, Pran.
15. 1969, *Aradhana*, dir. Shakti Samanta, prod. Shakti Samanta, starring Rajesh Khanna, Sharmila Tagore, Sujit Kumar.
16. 1972, *Amar Prem*, dir. Shakti Samanta, prod. Shakti Samanta, starring Rajesh Khanna, Sharmila Tagore, Vinod Mehra.
17. 1965, *Waqt*, dir. Yash Chopra, prod. B.R. Chopra, starring Balraj Sahni, Sharmila Tagore, Shashi Kapoor.
18. 1973, *Daag*, dir. Yash Chopra, prod. Yash Chopra, starring Sharmila Tagore, Rajesh Khanna, Raakhee.
19. 1976, *Kabhi Kabhie*, dir. Yash Chopra, prod. Yash Chopra, starring Amitabh Bachchan, Shashi Kapoor, Raakhee, Simi Garewal, Waheeda Rehman, Rishi Kapoor, Neetu Singh.
20. 1974, *Paap Aur Punya*, dir. Prayag Raj, prod. Shyam Kumar Shivdasani, starring Shashi Kapoor, Sharmila Tagore, Aruna Irani.
21. 'Yeh Sama, Sama Hai Ye Pyar Ka', lyr. Anand Bakshi, comp. Kalyanji–Anandji, artist Lata Mangeshkar.
22. 'Ni Sultana Re', lyr. Majrooh Sultanpuri, comp. R.D. Burman, artists Lata Mangeshkar, Mohammed Rafi.
23. 1969, *Pyar Ka Mausam*, dir. Nasir Hussain, prod. Nasir Hussain, starring Shashi Kapoor, Asha Parekh, Bharat Bhushan.
24. 'Kaise Kahen Hum Pyar Ne Humko', lyr. Neeraj, comp. S.D. Burman, artist Kishore Kumar.
25. 1971, *Sharmeelee*, dir. Samir Ganguly, prod. Subodh Mukherji, starring Shashi Kapoor, Raakhee, Nazir Hussain.

26. 1987, *Sammy and Rosie Get Laid*, dir. Stephen Frears, prod. Tim Bevan, Sarah Radclyffe, starring Shashi Kapoor, Frances Barber, Claire Bloom.
27. 1998, *Jinnah*, dir. Jamil Dehlavi, prod. Jamil Dehlavi, starring Christopher Lee, Shashi Kapoor, Maria Aitken.
28. 1998, *Side Streets*, dir. Tony Gerber, prod. Bruce Weiss, starring Valeria Golino, Shashi Kapoor, Shabana Azmi.
29. 1972, *Siddhartha*, dir. Conrad Rooks, prod. Conrad Rooks, starring Shashi Kapoor, Simi Garewal, Romesh Sharma.
30. 1981, *Kalyug*, dir. Shyam Benegal, prod. Shashi Kapoor, starring Shashi Kapoor, Rekha, Raj Babbar.
31. 1961, *Dharmputra*, dir. Yash Chopra, prod. B.R. Chopra, starring Shashi Kapoor, Mala Sinha, Rehman.

1

A STAR IS BORN
Shashi, Jennifer and the Movies

On 18 March 1938, at his home in Calcutta, a son was born to Prithviraj Kapoor—an actor in the studio, New Theatres. The boy was given the name Balbir Raj—in keeping with the Kapoor family tradition of adopting the word 'Raj' (or 'king') in its many variations. But Balbir's mother, Ramsarni Kapoor, was less than happy with the name. She began calling her son Shashi—or moonbeam—since her little boy was obsessed with the moon, spending long hours watching it.

Shashi Kapoor moved to Bombay, soon after he was born, to a large family house located on College Back Road in Matunga—an alley unofficially referred to as Hollywood Lane,[1] since, after Partition, many actors from Punjab had settled there. Today, it would be the equivalent of Yari Road in Versova and Lokhandwala in Andheri, with film stars and aspiring actors in every building.

Shashi grew up with his siblings and parents—although his father was often travelling—and spent his childhood being pampered by his mother and the other doting women of his household. The occasional admonishment he received was from his older brother, Raj Kapoor. Rishi Kapoor, Raj's son, says, 'My father did not distinguish between Shashi Uncle and Daboo (Rishi's older brother, Randhir Kapoor). He treated Shashi Uncle like his elder son.' However, not even Raj's rebukes could keep a young Shashi away from the cinema halls; he would skip his school, Don Bosco, to watch the latest films!

Six years after Shashi was born, Prithviraj established Prithvi Theatres. Shashi was instantly drawn to it; he played the role of Bharat in the company's first production, *Shakuntala*. The experience was compelling enough to persuade him that his heart was not in academic pursuits. By the time Shashi was a teenager, theatre became a driving force. In 1953, the wilful fifteen-year-old adolescent chose to quit school—a move that his father approved of—and joined Prithvi Theatres full time. This is where his real education began.

Being the son of the founder of a company did not mean much at Prithvi Theatres. Shashi had to find his way up the proverbial ladder. Filmmaker Dev Benegal, who worked as an assistant director in Shashi's home production, *Kalyug*,[2] says, 'One of the things Shashi mentioned to me was that when he was young, his father had told him, "Whatever you do, you have to start at the bottom. You need to lug the lights, lift the weights to really understand the nuts and bolts of creative work. You cannot come to me one fine day and assume that you can take over as the director!" Prithviraj didn't like people who came with a sense of entitlement. What was commendable was that he was training his kids in this ethic.' The coaching Shashi received at Prithvi Theatres and the respect he developed for those engaged in technical work—work that makes actors look good on stage and on screen—stayed with him throughout his professional career.

Shashi was at Prithvi Theatres from 1953 to 1960—the year Prithviraj was forced to close his company due to his poor health, after 2,662 shows across India. During that time, Shashi learned every aspect of theatre production and even performed small roles.

Whenever he could find time—in other words, when he was not touring with the theatre company—Shashi would drop by Raj's R.K. Films, where he'd observe the intricacies of filmmaking.

*

It was during his apprenticeship at Prithvi Theatres that Shashi Kapoor, through a quirk of fate, met the woman who would be his wife. Shashi's future sister-in-law, Felicity Kendal, writes in her autobiography, *White Cargo*, that one evening her sister, Jennifer Kendal—who was thirteen years older than her—went to the Royal Opera House in Bombay to catch a performance of *Deewaar* by Prithvi Theatres. Shashi was backstage and happened to look through the curtains; that's when he caught a glimpse of Jennifer. There she was 'dressed in a black and white polka-dotted summer dress with a halter neckline—daring—and she was pretty [...] fanning herself with her programme. Shashi [...] fell instantly in love.'[3]

Shashi Kapoor and Felicity Kendal in a scene from *Shakespeare Wallah*. Courtesy: Merchant-Ivory Productions.

Jennifer and Felicity's father, Geoffrey Kendal, who ran the Shakespeareana Theatre Company, has a slightly different account of this incident. In his autobiography, *The Shakespeare Wallah*, he sets the episode in Calcutta's Empire Theatre. According to him, the management company had made the mistake of double-booking the stage to Shakespeareana and Prithvi. A decision was eventually reached that the two companies would perform on alternate days. And it was on the evening of the Prithvi performance that Shashi saw Jennifer through the stage curtains. 'Not, of course, that I knew anything about this for some time,' Geoffrey says.[4]

After the show, Shashi introduced himself and took Jennifer backstage; she was four years older than him. Felicity writes: 'The next afternoon, I was sitting in a Chinese restaurant, watching Jennifer and Shashi fall in love over their noodles. They would stay together till she died, through thick and sometimes very thin [...] She had met in Shashi the man she wanted forever.'[5]

Soon after, as the Shakespeareana group fell short of actors, Shashi was asked to join the team, now based in Poona. Again, there is a slight discrepancy in the narration of facts here. Felicity writes that Jennifer wired Shashi to join the team, while Geoffrey presents a more plausible explanation of what could have happened—'I wrote to Prithviraj to ask if he could loan me Shashi from his company for a while.'[6] Shashi had never acted in English, but willingly joined the group in 1957. For five months, Jennifer walked him through the hoops of Shakespeare, Shaw and other English playwrights, helping him pronounce phrases that the young actor had never uttered or read. Sanjna Kapoor says, 'My father used to tell me how difficult it was learning the lines from Shakespeare—how terrifying the process used to be and how it felt like marbles were in his mouth. He just couldn't utter the words!'

Geoffrey may have welcomed a young Indian actor into his

fold. But he was not about to allow him into his family; he least expected his daughter to have intentions of marrying the boy. Geoffrey was extremely possessive of his children and he was particularly opposed to losing Jennifer, his star performer. In fits of protectiveness, he'd often ridicule Shashi and pour scorn over his accent. 'He would fight over Jennifer and he was often rude,' Shashi confesses to journalist Madhu Jain.[7]

The young lovers found themselves trying to escape Geoffrey's prying gaze. Sanjna says of her parents, 'When they were doing theatre, they were poor. They were under-slept and underfed and my father would tell me how they would be tormented by hunger while strolling down the streets—both my parents trying to decide if they could get half a paratha. Then, they would walk past a restaurant and there would be my grandfather, Geoffrey Kendal, having a huge meal with a beer. My father couldn't walk in. He was his employee and he was also stealing his daughter. So there was no way he could march into the storm.'

Geoffrey's obvious disregard for Shashi troubled Jennifer deeply, and she confronted her father. Then, she confided in Felicity, 'Daddy has told me that it isn't Shashi he objects to, or the fact that he is Indian, or that he is younger that I am [...] It is just that he doesn't want us to leave the company [...] I wish that he would understand that all children grow up and want to leave!'[8]

To add to Jennifer's woes, Shashi remained timid, self-conscious of his English and petrified of his parents. If their relationship progressed, it was because of the unstinted support of Shashi's sister-in-law (also an actor), Geeta Bali, and her husband (and Shashi's brother), Shammi Kapoor, who had learnt of the affair. It was a remarkable instance of life coming a full circle. Like Shammi, who had been prompted by Raj and his wife, Krishna, to marry Geeta, a diffident Shashi was instigated by Geeta and Shammi to bring Jennifer to Bombay and introduce her to his parents. But Shashi remained an apprehensive man. 'I chickened out because I thought I'd be thrashed,' Shashi laughs. 'So I compromised and took Jennifer to Shammiji's place instead and Geeta Bhabhi promptly fell in love with her. A true romantic herself, she'd loan us her car and a little money to go out for a meal and a drive.'[9] Eventually, at Shashi's behest, Shammi spoke to his parents about Jennifer and they grudgingly approved of the match.

Geoffrey, however, refused to shift his stance. He remained adamantly opposed to the relationship and set stern restrictions on his daughter. Finally, in a bid to claim her independence and move on, Jennifer, with Shashi, left his theatre troupe. For the patriarch, this was the ultimate let-down, and he was not about to take his daughter's desertion lightly. He watched, stern and wrathful, the day she left; it's a moment, frozen in time, of which Felicity gives a heartbreaking account:

> ...when we stood on the veranda that morning and Jennifer, red-eyed, threw her arms about his [Geoffrey's] neck, her tiny shoulders shaking with sobs, he stood, stiff and straight, his arms plastered to his sides, looking ahead and silent, until I pulled her away from him and hugged her into the waiting taxi. The look of bewilderment on Shashi's face at this appalling behaviour is something I will never forget.[10]

Jennifer and Shashi were now on their own, in a large, sometimes hostile world. They caught a flight to Singapore and Malaysia for a theatre show. But as luck would have it, the performances were cancelled, and they found themselves without any money. A desperate Shashi made a trunk call to India, and beseeched Raj for help, who speedily dispatched two economy tickets to Bombay. That was how Jennifer and Shashi reached the Kapoor family home in Matunga, and in July 1958, came to be married.

Geoffrey did not attend the wedding, but eventually reconciled with Jennifer when a son, Kunal, was born in 1960. The middle child, Karan, was born in 1962 and a daughter, Sanjna, five years later in 1967.

Those were heady years—though they came with specific challenges. 'Shashi once told me that when he got married to Jennifer, his room was a thoroughfare—he never really had any kind of privacy,' Sharmila Tagore says, recollecting the modest life of the man who would become a star. 'Fortunately, he had grown up with that kind of sharing and tolerance, in an atmosphere that demanded improvisation. It was part of him.'

Shashi, his wife and kids later moved to Altamount Road and eventually to Napean Sea Road in South Bombay, where Jennifer made every effort to give her children a normal life away from the glamour and over-the-top madness of the Hindi film industry. For one, the family had no television. When *Sikandar*,[11] which starred Prithviraj Kapoor, was broadcast, the family had to rent a TV set for a day. 'I must have been three, but I remember looking at the screen and saying, "Papa",' Sanjna says. 'Because my grandfather looked very much like my dad. I remember that very well.'

For another, on the days that Shashi was not travelling for shooting, Jennifer insisted that her family gather together in the mornings. 'Dad would have breakfast with us, no matter what time he came home from work,' says Kunal. 'We were up at 7 a.m., and at 7.30 a.m. we were at the table.'

Lastly, the children were taught to navigate the city like so many others. 'We travelled by BEST (Brihanmumbai Electric Supply and Transport) buses and local trains. It was something we grew to value—being normal people, almost anonymous,' Sanjna says. She also has strong memories of her mother dragging her to Bombay's chaotic Chor Bazaar: 'For me it was the greatest torture to be hauled there after school because my mother had to buy something—and it would never just be *one thing*. It would go on for four or five hours! But I also loved it because it was the one place in India where I was not Shashi Kapoor's daughter; I was

Jennifer Kendal Kapoor's child. Besides, my mother would always bribe me with dosas, idlis and vadas at an Udupi restaurant opposite Crawford Market!'

Given Jennifer's strict resolve to steer her household away from the excesses of stardom, Sanjna was taken by surprise when she realized that her father was a famous man. It happened rather unexpectedly, when Sanjna was two or three years old, and the family was in a car that had stopped at a traffic light. A motley group of street kids came by and started peering through the rolled-up glass windows. Soon, they began knocking frenetically, shouting, 'Shashi Kapoor, Shashi Kapoor!' 'I am told I turned to my father and asked, "Papa, how do they know your name?"' Sanjna laughs.

In spite of Jennifer's unsentimental approach to fame, it can't be denied that the family had to fine-tune its life to accommodate

Shashi Kapoor with his daughter, Sanjna, on the sets of *Heat and Dust*.
Photo credit: Mary Ellen Mark. Courtesy: Merchant-Ivory Productions.

Shashi's celebrity-dom. Sanjna says, 'I have never walked the streets of Bombay with my father in my entire life. That was impossible and I was completely aware of it.' Kunal, on his part, remembers rare early morning family visits to the zoo. 'We would have to get there before the zoo opened, and secure permission to visit half-an-hour before the crowds would descend. Towards the end of our appointment, fans would gather and start recognizing Dad.'

Finally, it was Goa that offered the sheltering cocoon that the Kapoors desired. The family had a home on Baga beach, and here, they'd walk, unnoticed. According to Felicity, it was her sister who first discovered the strand and even found the home she convinced Shashi to rent—one with a large heart painted on the tiled roof, so everyone came to call it the 'Love House'. Geoffrey, who came to vacation here often, referred to the neighbourhood as 'undoubtedly the most beautiful holiday place'.[12] This would be the family's vacation home every winter until Jennifer's death in September 1984.

'I think the greatest gift my parents ever gave us was the home in Goa before Goa became what it is now,' Sanjna says. 'I am sure my brothers will agree. We were normal, we were regular. The villagers tested us for more than a year until they accepted us. They didn't know who my father was.' She adds that Goa, at that time, had only a couple of movie theatres, and the local inhabitants—most of them Konkani fishermen—hardly watched Hindi films. 'Of course, they did eventually understand who Papa was. But then, they didn't care!'

*

While Jennifer Kendal Kapoor was alive, she maintained a strict watch over her husband's diet. This is the reason why, unlike the other Kapoor men, Shashi Kapoor stayed slim for the longest time. It was also why a lot of those around Shashi would feel sorry for him! 'I remember, when I worked with him, I would look at his food and say, "What's wrong with you, Shashi Uncle?"' Neetu Singh Kapoor tells me. 'One orange he would have and *thoda sa dahi* (a little bit of yogurt). That was his lunch. And he would say, "My wife will kill me if I eat anything more!"'

Writer and former head of the Film Finance Corporation (FFC), Anil Dharker—who first met Shashi for a BBC (British Broadcasting Corporation) radio interview, and soon became his close friend—also recalls the actor's food habits. 'I remember when Shashi and Jennifer had come to our house for dinner for the first time. Shashi went for a second helping. But when Jennifer very sternly said, "*Shashi!*" he quietly sat down.'

Then, there were the times Shashi would invite Anil over for lunch. 'I'd be offered a special kind of mutton, prepared by Raj Kapoor's cook, with ghee, salt and mirchi. It was called junglee gosht because, back in the day, when people went on shikar, they could only carry a few ingredients to make a wonderfully tasty dish! The problem was that it was also extremely rich because of the copious amounts of ghee used. So, Shashi would call me and say, "Look, Jennifer is out of town. Let's have this together." I would go over post-haste. The two of us would eat to our hearts' content and suffer for the next two days!'

But even when Jennifer imposed strict restrictions on his diet, Shashi enjoyed a couple of drinks of alcohol. Neetu Singh Kapoor says, 'I recall, *Kabhi Kabhie*[13] *ki party hui Bukhara main* (there was a party for *Kabhi Kabhie* at Bukhara) and all of us were there. Shashi Uncle had two or three drinks and became even cuter. The smile would not leave his face. I used to tell him, "You are the happiest drunk I know." Some people get angry after a few drinks. But Shashi Uncle seemed to become an even better person. Very *mast*! I adored him that way.'

*

On Sundays, the Kapoors of Napean Sea Road would take a family trip to Prithvi Jhonpra—Prithviraj Kapoor's residence in the Janki Kutir area of Juhu. Prithviraj's neighbour was the poet Kaifi Azmi. And one person, in particular, would get terribly excited about the Sunday visits of Shashi Kapoor—Kaifi's daughter, Shabana Azmi. She had a big crush on the Hindi movie star. She tells me, 'My mother (the actress, Shaukat Azmi) had known Shashi since he was seven years old because of her association with Prithviraj Kapoor and Prithvi Theatres. So yes, the families were close. I was a crazy fan of Shashi. When I was around twelve or thirteen, I would save all my pocket money to buy his black-and-white photographs every week from a vendor near my school at Grant Road. I'd shyly give Shashi the photograph when he'd come over and he would autograph it for me.' Years later, Shabana and Shashi would act together in eight films.

In 1986, at the height of her political and social activism, Shabana went on a hunger strike along with documentary filmmaker, Anand Patwardhan. Their organization, Nivara Haqq, wanted alternate housing for Colaba's slum-dwellers, whose homes had been demolished to build a hostel for ministers. On the fifth day of the strike, Shabana's blood pressure began to drop; there was chaos all around. Shashi rushed to see Shabana and tried understanding the organization's demands more thoroughly. Then, he went to meet the chief minister of Maharashtra. Shabana says, 'He told the chief minister, "The film industry always rallies around you when you need its support to battle natural disasters or calamities. Yet, when one of our prominent members goes on a hunger strike, the government takes no notice."' Promptly, the chief minister called the state's housing minister who, in turn, told the demonstrators that after Shashi's intervention, the government felt compelled to accept their demands.

Shabana says, 'I clambered up to the stage. But before I could say, "Nivara Haqq wants to thank Shashi Kapoor", I saw him quietly slip away into one of Colaba's back alleys. He wished to claim no credit. Such generosity is typical of Shashi.'

Bombay-based journalist, Sameera Khan, also remembers Shashi's kindness. Sameera and her parents were the Kapoors' neighbours in Atlas Apartments, Napean Sea Road. The Khans were the only Muslim family in the building. In January 1993, during the Bombay riots, the Khan family was forced to flee for safety. 'We had no support from Atlas' society and there was a growing sense of unease,' Sameera says. 'While we were away, the society held a meeting to pass a resolution that henceforth no Muslims would be allowed to rent or buy flats in the building. The only person to vociferously protest and walk out was Shashi Kapoor. He may not remember me or my family, but every time I see him, I feel insanely hopeful.'

Notes

1. According to an entry in the *Encyclopaedia of Hindi Cinema*, edited by Gulzar, Govind Nihalani and Saibal Chatterjee (Bombay: Popular Prakashan, 2003).
2. 1981, *Kalyug*, dir. Shyam Benegal prod. Shashi Kapoor, starring Shashi Kapoor, Rekha, Raj Babbar.
3. Felicity Kendal, *White Cargo* (London: Michael Joseph, 1998), p. 157.
4. Geoffrey Kendal, *The Shakespeare Wallah: An Autobiography* (London: Sidgwick & Jackson, 1986), p. 133.
5. Felicity Kendal, *White Cargo* (London: Michael Joseph, 1998), p. 157.
6. Geoffrey Kendal, *The Shakespeare Wallah: An Autobiography* (London: Sidgwick & Jackson, 1986), p. 133.
7. Madhu Jain, *The Kapoors: The First Family of Indian Cinema* (New Delhi: Penguin, 2005), p. 227.
8. Felicity Kendal, *White Cargo* (London: Michael Joseph, 1998), p. 163.
9. Shammi Kapoor, 'The Kapoor Family Website', in <http://www.junglee.org.in/jennifer.html>, accessed on 11 January 2015.
10. Felicity Kendal, *White Cargo* (London: Michael Joseph, 1998), p. 172.
11. 1941, *Sikandar*, dir. Sohrab Modi, prod. Sohrab Modi, starring Prithviraj Kapoor, Sohrab Modi, Zahur Raja.

12. Geoffrey Kendal, *The Shakespeare Wallah: An Autobiography* (London: Sidgwick & Jackson, 1986), p. 158.

13. 1976, *Kabhi Kabhie*, dir. Yash Chopra, prod. Yash Chopra, starring Amitabh Bachchan, Shashi Kapoor, Raakhee, Simi Garewal, Waheeda Rehman, Rishi Kapoor, Neetu Singh.

2

THE ASCENT
Shashi and the Early Films

Shashi Kapoor's first film appearance was not as a dapper hero in a Merchant–Ivory production, but, in fact, as a pudgy adolescent in a commercial film. In the celebrated Indian movie, *Awara*,[1] directed by his elder brother, Raj Kapoor, a smooth-faced Shashi—already displaying the wide-eyed charm of his adult self—played a younger version of the character portrayed by Raj. Shashi was thirteen at the time of the film's release, while Raj was twenty-seven. The film also starred their father, Prithviraj Kapoor, as the judge who would abandon his pregnant wife, upset that she had been raped by the dacoit who had kidnapped her.

Clearly, *Awara* shared strong parallels with the Ram–Sita–Ravana narrative, imbued with a generous dose of melodrama and bathos. Its plot was also built around whimsy and coincidence—the young Shashi's character would lose the girl he loved, only to meet her again in adult life; he'd also get adopted by Jagga Daku, the same man who had once kidnapped his mother!

While Shashi is credited with smaller roles in a couple of other films of that time, it is *Awara* that his fans keep returning to—for the child actor with melting eyes, besides the foot-tapping songs and the smoldering romantic moments between Raj and Rita (played by Nargis). It is, therefore, recognized as the film that 'launched' Shashi—for, already, the young actor was showing immense promise, displaying a flair for drama and a keen aptitude for performance.

*

When an adult Shashi Kapoor decided to join the Indian film industry, the reasons weren't exactly starry-eyed; he had to support his family. 'I came into the movies as an actor for money,' Shashi Kapoor tells Rachel Dwyer, a writer and professor of Indian cinema, in an interview for her book. 'I liked theatre, but there was no money in it.'[2] Kunal Kapoor corroborates this: 'After I was born, my father realized that he had to supplement his income to fund the lifestyle his family wished to enjoy. You see, Mum read a lot of books—and, as we know, books are expensive!'

Once the decision was made—that Shashi would become part of the film industry—the real struggle began. While Shashi had pedigree—he was the son of the pioneering Prithviraj Kapoor, and the brother of two already illustrious actors, Shammi Kapoor and Raj Kapoor—he had limited film experience. Like the thousands in Bombay looking for film work, Shashi had to spend hours visiting directors and studios, distributing portfolio pictures, and hanging outside coffee shops to get noticed by busy producers.

Finally, Shashi got his first break. He was asked to act in a social melodrama, *Char Diwari*,[3] with Nanda as the female lead. Nanda was a year younger than Shashi, but already, she was a household name and a star with a considerable fan-following, having acted in over twenty-five films, including some huge hits— among them, *Dhool Ka Phool*[4] and *Kanoon*.[5] The story goes that Nanda, the film idol, decided to act with Shashi, the novice, at the behest of Raj—who displayed classic signs of brotherly protectiveness when he asked Nanda to watch over Shashi since she was his 'senior'. Nanda, subsequently, went on to reveal the nature of the conversation: 'Raj told me, "[Shashi] is not my brother. He is my son. [Acting] is a very new experience for him."'[6]

Char Diwari did not fare well at the box office, even though it had lilting music composed by Salil Chowdhury—including that evergreen song sung by Mukesh, 'Kaise Manaoon Piyawa'.[7] Soon after, Shashi went on to act in two more films with Nanda—*Mehndi Lagi Mere Haath*[8] and *Mohabbat Isko Kahete Hain*.[9] Both failed.

It was as though Shashi's career was fated to combust too soon, and with that, Nanda's. But then came the year 1965, and the film, *Jab Jab Phool Khile*[10]—a love story set in Kashmir. Its novel theme (back then) of rupturing class boundaries, and its hugely popular songs (including 'Pardesiyon Se Na Ankhiyan Milana'[11] and 'Na Na Karte Pyar'[12]), captured the imagination of the audience. The film became a surprise hit, and suddenly, Shashi was an actor in demand along with Nanda! The pair would work together in four more films—a total of eight through the 1960s.

After an uncertain beginning, the second half of the 1960s firmly cemented Shashi's career. The actor appeared in a number of films (apart from those with Nanda)—*Pyar Ka Mausam*[13] with Asha Parekh, and the comedy *Pyar Kiye Jaa*,[14] in which the twenty-eight-year-old actor outshone his effervescent brother, Shammi, performing the smoothest and most energetic of dance moves, including the iconic twist, to the song, 'Kehne Ki Nahin Baat'.[15] The premise of the song—and indeed, the whole film—is entirely silly, but it is the kind of mindless fun that places huge demands on actors. Shashi rose to the challenge and remains a delight to watch.

Then, there was Prakash Mehra's first feature, *Haseena Maan Jayegi*[16]—another scatterbrained but harmless film—in which Shashi acted opposite Babita (who would marry his nephew, Randhir Kapoor, two years later). The movie is punctuated with comedy tracks starring Johnny Walker and Ameeta; is jam-packed with songs composed by Kalyanji–Anandji—including the memorable 'Chale The Saath Milke'[17] and the incredibly romantic 'Bekhudi Main Sanam';[18] and presents the rising star, Shashi, in a zany double role—he's both Kamal and Rakesh. That's not all. In a hilarious and cleverly choreographed song, 'Suno Suno',[19] one of Shashi's characters, while describing the conclusions of his research on the kinds of women populating the world, is made to dress in drag; there's a terrific segment where Shashi wears a tawaif's outfit and dances to parodies of hit Hindi film songs. Shashi is so energetic in this song sequence—running rings, bounding and

Shashi Kapoor: A star in the making. Courtesy: Merchant-Ivory Productions.

working his feet—that one is reminded strongly of Shammi's *Junglee*,[20] *Professor*[21] and *Janwar*[22]—except that Shashi's lithe body frame makes him a lot more agile and fluid than his brother! It must be admitted that *Haseena Maan Jayegi* is a film of no consequence—it makes no attempt to explain why the two Shashis look alike; offers no twist in the tale to suggest that Kamal and Rakesh are long-lost twins; and makes us believe that the only rationale guiding the existence of doppelgängers is to further perplex a terribly confused heroine. But the song, 'Suno Suno' remains a special treat for Shashi fans.

If the 1960s were a landmark decade in Shashi's life, it was also because this period defined three other connections in his life— with the filmmaker, Yash Chopra, who became Shashi's close friend; with the actress, Sharmila Tagore, who had just begun to make a transition from Bengali classics to out-and-out commercial films; and with the legendary director, Bimal Roy, who cast the actor in two films (though both failed at the box office).

The Early Yash Chopra Films

Yash Chopra's first meeting with Shashi Kapoor, likely towards the end of the 1950s, was unexpected and surprisingly brief. It's said that Yash spotted Shashi as he approached Gaylord's, the legendary restaurant in Bombay's Churchgate area, once frequented by struggling actors. Possibly intrigued by the young Shashi's charm and good looks, the renowned director invited him to his table. After a quick conversation—during which time Shashi naturally revealed his family background—Yash advised the aspiring actor to visit his brother B.R. Chopra's office in Kardar Studios, which Shashi did without delay. Here, it's said, Yash narrated the story of his new film, to be produced by his brother, to an astonished Shashi. This was how *Dharmputra*[23] found its star.

Quick on the heels of the huge hit, *Dhool Ka Phool*—a film with a social conscience—Yash's second cinematic foray,

Dharmputra, based on a novel by Acharya Chatursen Shastri, chose to explore the fraught terrain of Hindu–Muslim conflict in a newly-Independent India through the story of a young Muslim couple; the two leave their baby, born out of wedlock, with Hindu friends, only to discover years later that their Muslim son is now a Hindu fanatic.

Shashi, who was twenty-three at the time of the film's release, played the challenging role of an overzealous Hindu who knew nothing about his biological roots. Besides agonizing over his character, Shashi also found himself wrestling with the conventions that guided Hindi cinema. During an interview with Rachel Dwyer, Shashi speaks of Yash's loquaciousness (often an issue even when journalists met the director); how one subject spun into another; and that, at the end of it, the director and the actor found themselves at loggerheads. Shashi, a reluctant star of Hindi cinema, still had youthful ideals—one of them being that he could not sing songs in films; Yash, on the other hand, was not about to change a formula that worked. 'I took my part too seriously,' Shashi admits to Rachel. Finally, the 'sophisticated and Western' actor had to relent to his director's command. 'One song was revolutionary,' Shashi says in his interview, 'and one, romantic.'[24]

The romantic song, 'Bhool Sakta Hai Bhala Kaun'[25]—a small, albeit touching, diversion in an otherwise tightly focused story—has Shashi's Dilip Rai singing in Mahendra Kapoor's quiet, dreamy voice to his love interest in the film, Meena (played by Indrani Mukherjee), seated across him. Shashi wears a pencil-thin moustache—a touch that makes him even more dashing—and recites a love poem his character has written; the beauty of the scene is enhanced by the film's black-and-white imagery.

Dharmputra—which went on to win the National Award (1961) for the best Hindi film—was a washout at the box office, perhaps because the audiences were not interested in a story about religious divides fracturing a young nation, so soon after Partition. The film's failure was a huge loss for B.R. Chopra, whose banner had otherwise backed very successful films.

Box office verdicts aside, it was *Dharmputra* that fortified a strong friendship between Yash, Shashi and also Deven Verma, who acted as the protagonist's younger brother in the film. Later, according to Pamela Chopra, Shashi and Yash came forward to assist Deven with his wedding to Rupa Ganguly (the daughter of Ashok Kumar), when there was strong opposition from her family.

How does one explain Shashi's friendship with Yash? According to Rachel, their association was buoyed by their backgrounds. 'Shashi was very Punjabi, despite the Western touches that came from Jennifer. Such "Punjabiness" typified the Kapoor family and the Chopra household; it was evident in the food, the lifestyle and the sociability. If there was a divide between Shashi and Yashji, it was because Yashji didn't drink.'

Rachel adds that Yash shared with Shashi and Jennifer their interest in the arts—one that went beyond the ambit of commercial Hindi cinema. 'Yashji was a lifelong member of IPTA (Indian People's Theatre Association) and was a huge fan of theatre,' she says. 'People always assume Pam and he were filmy, but I have watched, with them, quite a few obscure movies and art-house cinema. Such curiosity defined the couple.' This might explain why Shashi tells Rachel, 'He [Yash] was the only director apart from [Ismail] Merchant and [James] Ivory that Jennifer would have home.'[26]

Despite the failure of *Dharmputra*, B.R. Chopra gave his brother, Yash, another chance with *Waqt*[27]—the banner's first colour film and also one with a dazzling multi-star cast. In the movie, a successful merchant, Lala Kedarnath (Balraj Sahni), gets parted from his family—his wife and three young sons—after a devastating earthquake (a reference to a massive earthquake that hit Quetta in 1935). The sons grow up separately and lead vastly different lives—with one becoming a sophisticated thief, another stumbling into a world of entitlement and privilege, and a third following the straight and narrow path of hard work and diligence, at least initially. Their lives connect through their love interests, and finally, the family unites in an over-the-top scene—a complete tear-jerker—in a courtroom.

Given the structural complexity of the narrative, the film has a huge cast! The oldest son—the gangster, Raju—is portrayed by Raaj Kumar, who gets to say the cult favourite line: '*Chenoy Seth, jinke apne ghar sheeshe ke hon woh doosron ke gharron par patthar nahi phenka karte.*' ('Chenoy Seth, those who live in houses made of glass do not throw stones at the homes of others.') The middle son—the prosperous lawyer, Ravi—is played by Sunil Dutt, while Shashi stars as Munna, the youngest—who becomes a driver to support his mother, and is then compelled to make dubious choices to cure her of a crippling illness. As for the love interests, Achala Sachdev plays Kedarnath's wife, Laxmi (with Balraj Sahni's Kedarnath singing Manna Dey's unforgettable 'Ae Meri Zohra Jabeen'[28] to her); Sadhana plays Meena—Ravi's paramour—only to find Raju getting infatuated by her; and for the first time, Shashi is paired with Sharmila Tagore, fresh from the success of her debut Hindi film, *Kashmir Ki Kali*.[29]

Waqt was not only a major box office hit, but also became an industry standard. Lavish sets; the latest cars; good-looking, fashionably dressed stars; catchy songs; as also, countless subplots involving families separated by extraneous circumstances became all the rage. Through the 1970s and 1980s, the Hindi film industry would concoct many such narratives, and these films would always be packed with the top stars of the time—including, in many instances, Shashi.

The Early Sharmila Tagore Films

Sharmila Tagore remembers the first time she met Shashi Kapoor— when he dropped by the sets of Shakti Samanta's *Kashmir Ki Kali*.

Shashi had come to see his brother, Shammi Kapoor, who was playing a lead role in the film. 'Jennifer (Kendal Kapoor) and Shashi had seen *Apur Sansar*[30] and had liked my performance,' Sharmila tells me. 'I had seen Shashi in *Prem Patra*.[31] And I was in love with him! *Bahut handsome tha usme.* (He was very handsome in it.) All I remember is that he was blind in the film. And that, while Sadhana folded saris in one scene, Shashi sat in a chair looking gorgeous.'

Shashi's unannounced visit to the sets of *Kashmir Ki Kali* unnerved eighteen-year-old Sharmila. 'We were shooting the song "Isharon Isharon Main Dil Lenewale",[32] and I said to myself, "Oh my god! This is Shashi Kapoor." And I couldn't work. Shakti finally asked him to leave.'

By the time *Waqt* was finalized, Sharmila, slightly older and more experienced, was a lot more comfortable with the young actor. Besides, the demands of the box office required a Sharmila–Shashi romantic pairing. 'When *Waqt* came by, we happened to get the attention of the younger generation,' Sharmila says. 'Most certainly we filled a need and we did this successfully. There's a scene where we sing on a boat—"Din Hai Bahar Ke"[33]—and everything, right down to my clothes, came to be appreciated.'

Shashi and Sharmila became symbols of a young couple in love—akin to Rishi Kapoor–Neetu Singh a decade later—and the pairing became a norm not only in Yash Chopra multi-starrers but also across several other movies. Sharmila and Shashi, consequently, would appear together in ten films, including *Aamne Saamne*,[34] *Suhana Safar*,[35] *Aa Gale Lag Jaa*[36] and the National Award-winning *New Delhi Times*.[37]

The two not only became popular co-stars, but also actors who grew together, taking cues from one another. Sharmila says, 'Shashi would constantly tease me because I would argue a lot with the directors on the sets. Each time, he'd remind me to get on with it—don't bicker, just do it! This is what I've learnt from him. When you are doing a film for money or to help a friend out, be clear about the motives and then finish what needs to be done. When you come to the set, and are aware of the limitations of the script or the director, don't expect pigs to fly.'

Sharmila also came to appreciate Shashi's work ethic. 'He always listened to his director and *always* came to the sets on time,' Sharmila says, hinting at the fact that she stopped accepting films with the raging heart-throb of the late 1960s, Rajesh Khanna, because of the actor's tardy behaviour. 'And, of course, second to arrive would be Mr (Amitabh) Bachchan.'

Most of all, Sharmila recalls Shashi's sparkling sense of humour through good times and bad. She says, 'We were shooting *Suhana Safar*, and there was a scene where I was supposed to drive downhill, and Shashi was to jump out of the way. But something went wrong—I just could not control the clutch and brake and sped into a culvert. While the poor light man holding a reflector fell, Shashi remained unscathed. Later, he quipped, "Do that again, and Jennifer will come to you with three children and say she doesn't have money for milk!" He could always joke, and yet remain cordial and respectful.'

Over the years, Shashi's family and Sharmila's—their respective spouses and children—grew close. It helped that both households lived in South Bombay, away from the noise and glamour of the Hindi film industry. It also helped that Shashi and Sharmila, over years of filmmaking, had developed a bond that was warm, even mischievous. Sharmila says, 'By the time I met Tiger (her future husband and cricketer, the nawab of Pataudi) I had cultivated the habit of saying, at once, "alvida" and "khuda hafiz". And Shashi would tease me by saying, "Half is his and half is mine!" I always had a soft spot for Shashi. I remember his eyelashes.'

The Bimal Roy Films

In the late 1950s, Shashi Kapoor ran into the legendary filmmaker Bimal Roy—known for such classics as *Do Bigha Zamin*,[38]

Madhumati,[39] and *Sujata*[40]—at an event organized by *Filmfare*.
Shashi had known Bimal since his childhood, and after the meeting,
was invited to meet the director at Mohan Studios.

When Shashi arrived, he found many of the filmmaker's
assistants (and future directors)—Gulzar, Hrishikesh Mukherjee
and Basu Bhattacharya (who would later marry Bimal's daughter,
Rinki, much to Bimal's chagrin)—outside his office. Shashi even
spotted Dharmendra—at that point, much like him, a struggling
actor. Word was that Bimal was casting for the two films he had in
mind—*Prem Patra* and *Bandini*[41]—and Shashi guessed that
Dharmendra and he were in the running.

When he was summoned, Shashi nervously went into a room
for a meeting with Bimal. The director came straight to the point,
and in Hindi, laced with a thick Bengali accent, said:
'Shashibabu...*ek picture banayga* [I want to make a picture]...I
want you.'[42]

Shashi, of course, was delighted. He had no idea which of the
two films he would be cast in—but it hardly mattered. He was
happy to take what he got.

It turned out that Shashi—considered a good fit for romantic
roles—had secured *Prem Patra*. And Dharmendra eventually played
a supporting role in *Bandini*. What if the casting had been reversed
by Bimal? What if Dharmendra had played the visually-challenged
Arun, and Shashi had become the kindly prison doctor whose love
would remain unrequited? One can only speculate if the actors'
careers would had played out differently...

In any case, some time after making his casting decision, Bimal
asked Shashi how much money he wanted for the role. It was an
awkward question, but Shashi told him that that he was being
paid Rs 25,000 by B.R. and Yash Chopra for *Dharmputra*. In an
essay, Shashi writes: 'He was surprised and asked, "Will they pay
you so much?" I said, "Yes, they are big producers." He replied,
"Alright, I'll pay you the same."'[43] And with that, shooting began.

Prem Patra is a quietly made film—a story of two medical students, Arun (Shashi Kapoor) and Kavita (Sadhana), who are attracted to each other, but then fall apart because of a misunderstanding involving a love letter. Arun's eventual betrothal to Saroj (Seema Deo) who, unbeknownst to the man, is Kavita's cousin, leads to a giant tussle between appearances and reality, between what one sees and what is—with the theme being taken to a literal denouement when Arun turns blind.

Bimal Roy takes his time to resolve the misunderstandings—on account of which the film can feel a tad bit long. But an otherwise protracted story is buoyed by the lilting music of Salil Chowdhury ('Yeh Mere Andhere Ujale Na Hote',[44] 'Do Akhiyan Jhuki Jhuki',[45] among other songs), and lead actors who look stunning—the crisp black-and-white cinematography bringing them to life in every frame. Shashi looks especially handsome, first in his neatly clipped moustache, and later, as he walks in dark glasses. But as was the case with the actor's other early films, *Prem Patra* failed at the box office.

However, this verdict did not discourage Bimal. As Shashi recalls, Bimal felt guilty about the failure of *Prem Patra* and would often tell the actor, '*Phirse tumko lega…hum kaam karega ek saaath.* [I will take you again…we will work together.] You are still one of us at Bimal Roy Productions.'[46]

True to his word, Bimal cast Shashi yet again—this time, in *Benazir*,[47] a film produced by Bimal's banner and directed by S. Khalil. This time, too, there was an awkward conversation about how much Shashi expected to be paid. Shashi writes, 'I told [Bimal] that I needed money. I did not have financial support from my brothers or anyone else, and had a family, and living at Olympus at Altamount Road was expensive.'[48] Shashi then told Bimal that he was getting paid Rs 1,00,000 for acting in *Waqt*—once again letting B.R. Chopra's banner set the benchmark. Shashi remembers: '[Bimal] said, "I don't believe it," and I asked him to check it up. He said, "No, I will pay you the same…that's it."'[49]

In *Benazir*—a film that unspools in Lucknow, and belongs to
the 'Muslim social' genre—Shashi, as Anwar, plays younger brother
to Ashok Kumar's Nawab. The story goes that both siblings, at
different points, fall in love with Benazir, a theatre actress and
dancing girl, played by Meena Kumari. When the brothers' liaisons
with the same woman come to light, jealousies and
misunderstandings erupt. *Benazir* is a beautifully told narrative,
and Bimal Roy's second favourite music composer, S.D. Burman
(his favourite being Salil Chowdhury), makes it doubly poetic
with lyrical songs including 'Dil Mein Ek Jaane Tamanna',[50]
where Shashi's Anwar sings in Mohammed Rafi's voice. By the
time *Benazir* was being made, Shashi had clearly become
comfortable singing romantic numbers for films.

Even though *Benazir* met with the same fate as *Prem Patra*,
Shashi's youthful looks, his smile and even the couple of crooked
teeth that would charmingly peek out when he'd grin came to be
remembered.

Shashi, on his part, found himself especially appreciative of a
principled Bimal when, towards the end of the 1960s, he found
himself caught in a rather disagreeable situation. Producer
N.C. Sippy had signed him on to play the lead role in *Anand*[51]—
but as we know, the film has Rajesh Khanna as the protagonist
and Amitabh Bachchan as a supporting character. What happened
along the way? Shashi had this to tell *The Sunday Guardian*
reporter: 'Yes, I was [offered a role in *Anand*]. But the first day I
went for the shoot, I was informed that I was not required, so I
came back. I returned my signing amount to producer N.C. Sippy
and very well understood that Hrishikesh Mukherjee was never as
noble a soul as Bimal Roy was.'[52]

Notes

1. 1951, *Awara*, dir. Raj Kapoor, prod. Raj Kapoor, starring Prithviraj Kapoor, Raj Kapoor, Nargis, Shashi Kapoor.
2. Rachel Dwyer, *Yash Chopra: Fifty Years of Indian Cinema* (New Delhi: Roli, 2002), p. 54.
3. 1961, *Char Diwari*, dir. Krishan Chopra, prod. Jagan Prasad Sharma, starring Shashi Kapoor, Nanda, Manmohan Krishna.
4. 1959, *Dhool Ka Phool*, dir. Yash Chopra, prod. B.R. Chopra, starring Mala Sinha, Nanda, Rajendra Kumar.
5. 1960, *Kanoon*, dir. B.R. Chopra, prod. B.R. Chopra, starring Rajendra Kumar, Ashok Kumar, Nanda.
6. Quoted in Madhu Jain, *The Kapoors: The First Family of Indian Cinema* (New Delhi: Penguin, 2005), p. 230.
7. 'Kaise Manaoon Piyawa', lyr. Shailendra, comp. Salil Chowdhury, artist Mukesh.
8. 1962, *Mehndi Lagi Mere Haath*, dir. Suraj Prakash, prod. Hiren Khera, starring Ashok Kumar, Nanda, Shashi Kapoor.
9. 1965, *Mohabbat Isko Kahete Hain*, dir. Akhtar Mirza, starring Nanda, Shashi Kapoor, Ramesh Deo.
10. 1965, *Jab Jab Phool Khile*, dir. Suraj Prakash, prod. Chetan K., starring Shashi Kapoor, Nanda, Agha.
11. 'Pardesiyon Se Na Ankhiyan Milana', lyr. Anand Bakshi, comp. Kalyanji–Anandji, artists Lata Mangeshkar, Mohammed Rafi.
12. 'Na Na Karte Pyar', lyr. Anand Bakshi, comp. Kalyanji–Anandji, artist Mohammed Rafi.
13. 1969, *Pyar Ka Mausam*, dir. Nasir Hussain, prod. Nasir Hussain, starring Shashi Kapoor, Asha Parekh, Bharat Bhushan.
14. 1966, *Pyar Kiye Jaa*, dir. C.V. Sridhar, starring Shashi Kapoor, Kalpana, Mumtaz.
15. 'Kehne Ki Nahin Baat', lyr. Rajendra Krishan, comp. Laxmikant–Pyarelal, artist Mohammed Rafi.
16. 1968, *Haseena Maan Jayegi*, dir. Prakash Mehra, prod. S.M. Abbas, starring Shashi Kapoor, Babita, Johnny Walker.
17. 'Chale The Saath Milke', lyr. Akhtar Romani, comp. Kalyanji–Anandji, artist Mohammed Rafi.
18. 'Bekhudi Main Sanam', lyr. Akhtar Romani, comp. Kalyanji–Anandji, artists Mohammed Rafi, Lata Mangeshkar.
19. 'Suno Suno', lyr. Prakash Mehra, comp. Kalyanji–Anandji, artist Mohammed Rafi.

20. 1961, *Junglee*, dir. Subodh Mukherji, prod. Subodh Mukherji, starring Shammi Kapoor, Saira Banu, Shashikala.
21. 1962, *Professor*, dir. Lekh Tandon, prod. F.C. Mehra, starring Shammi Kapoor, Kalpana, Lalita Pawar.
22. 1965, *Janwar*, dir. Bhappi Sonie, prod. S. Hardip, starring Shammi Kapoor, Rajshree, Rehman.
23. 1961, *Dharmputra*, dir. Yash Chopra, prod. B.R. Chopra, starring Mala Sinha, Shashi Kapoor, Rehman.
24. Rachel Dwyer, *Yash Chopra: Fifty Years of Indian Cinema* (New Delhi: Roli, 2002), p. 54.
25. 'Bhool Sakta Hai Bhala Kaun', lyr. Sahir Ludhianvi, comp. Dutta Naik, artist Mahendra Kapoor.
26. Rachel Dwyer, *Yash Chopra: Fifty Years of Indian Cinema* (New Delhi: Roli, 2002), p. 226.
27. 1965, *Waqt*, dir. Yash Chopra, prod. B.R. Chopra, starring Balraj Sahni, Sharmila Tagore, Shashi Kapoor.
28. 'Ae Meri Zohra Jabeen', lyr. Sahir Ludhianvi, comp. Ravi Shankar Sharma, artist Manna Dey.
29. 1964, *Kashmir Ki Kali*, dir. Shakti Samanta, prod. Shakti Samanta, starring Shammi Kapoor, Sharmila Tagore, Pran.
30. 1959, *Apur Sansar*, dir. Satyajit Ray, prod. Satyajit Ray, starring Soumitra Chatterjee, Sharmila Tagore, Alok Chakravarty.
31. 1962, *Prem Patra*, dir. Bimal Roy, prod. Bimal Roy, starring Shashi Kapoor, Sadhana, Seema Deo.
32. 'Isharon Isharon Main Dil Lenewale', lyr. S.H. Bihari, comp. O.P. Nayyar, artists Mohammed Rafi, Asha Bhosle.
33. 'Din Hai Bahar Ke', lyr. Sahir Ludhianvi, comp. Ravi, artists Asha Bhosle, Mahindra Kapoor.
34. 1967, *Aamne Saamne*, dir. Suraj Prakash, prod. Suraj Prakash, starring Shashi Kapoor, Sharmila Tagore, Prem Chopra.
35. 1970, *Suhana Safar*, dir. Vijay, prod. R.C. Kumar, starring Shashi Kapoor, Sharmila Tagore, Lalita Pawar.
36. 1973, *Aa Gale Lag Jaa*, dir. Manmohan Desai, prod. A.K. Nadiadwala, starring Shashi Kapoor, Sharmila Tagore, Shatrughan Sinha.
37. 1986, *New Delhi Times*, dir. Ramesh Sharma, prod. P.K. Tiwari, starring Shashi Kapoor, Sharmila Tagore, Om Puri.
38. 1953, *Do Bigha Zamin*, dir. Bimal Roy, prod. Bimal Roy, starring Balraj Sahni, Nirupa Roy, Nazir Hussain.
39. 1958, *Madhumati*, dir. Bimal Roy, prod. Bimal Roy, starring Dilip Kumar, Vyjayanthimala, Johnny Walker.

40. 1959, *Sujata*, dir. Bimal Roy, prod. Bimal Roy, starring Nutan, Sunil Dutt, Lalita Pawar.
41. 1963, *Bandini*, dir. Bimal Roy, prod. Bimal Roy, starring Nutan, Ashok Kumar, Dharmendra.
42. Quoted in Shashi Kapoor, 'Memories of Dada', *Bimal Roy: A Man of Silence*, edited by Rinki Bhattacharya (New Delhi: HarperCollins, 1994), p. 136.
43. *Ibid.*, p. 137.
44. 'Yeh Mere Andhere Ujale Na Hote', lyr. Rajinder Krishan, comp. Salil Chowdhury, artists Lata Mangeshkar, Talat Mahmood.
45. 'Do Akhiyan Jhuki Jhuki', lyr. Rajinder Krishan, comp. Salil Chowdhury, artists Lata Mangeshkar, Mukesh.
46. Quoted in Shashi Kapoor, 'Memories of Dada', *Bimal Roy: A Man of Silence*, edited by Rinki Bhattacharya (New Delhi: HarperCollins, 1994) p. 138.
47. 1964, *Benazir*, dir. S. Khalil, prod. Bimal Roy, starring Ashok Kumar, Meena Kumari, Shashi Kapoor.
48. Shashi Kapoor, 'Memories of Dada', *Bimal Roy: A Man of Silence*, edited by Rinki Bhattacharya (New Delhi: HarperCollins, 1994), p. 138.
49. *Ibid.*
50. 'Dil Mein Ek Jaane Tamanna', lyr. Shakeel Badayuni, comp. S.D. Burman, artist Mohammed Rafi.
51. 1971, *Anand*, dir. Hrishikesh Mukherjee, prod. Hrishikesh Mukherjee, N.C. Sippy, starring Rajesh Khanna, Amitabh Bachchan, Sumita Sanyal.
52. Ranjan Das Gupta, 'Shammi was a Better Romantic Hero: Shashi Kapoor', *The Sunday Guardian*, 22 March 2014.

3

CHALO AMERICA
Shashi, Merchant-Ivory and Rooks

James Ivory remembers it clearly. In November 1961, he had arrived in a wintry Bombay, en route to a tiny village in Gujarat, where he planned to shoot a feature film, *Devgar*—written by the anthropologist, Geetal Steed.[1] His New York-based friend, Ismail Merchant, was planning to produce it, and Sidney Meyers was to become the director. Ismail hoped to cast Shashi Kapoor and Leela Naidu, a young French–Indian actress, in lead roles, and get veteran actress, Durga Khote, to play the elderly mother.

But first, Ismail wanted James to meet Shashi. And so, one evening, James and Ismail headed to the Cricket Club of India for a film function. As James recalls, 'I remember going down the long corridor—a tented corridor, as it were—to some place where Shashi was supposed to be. But just at that moment, Shashi and Jennifer emerged. So, we had our meeting right there, in that enclosed passageway. Jennifer was very nice and welcoming. Ismail had told Shashi about me, and the actor was friendly in his usual way. That was the first time we met—he must have been twenty-three then—and I was struck by how extraordinarily handsome he was.'

At an earlier time, under equally unusual circumstances, Ismail had met Shashi; accompanied by an Australian woman who worked at an advertising agency, he had gatecrashed a party that the young actor was hosting at his house for a few film journalists. Ismail—who passed away after a brief illness in 2005—writes in his autobiography, *My Passage from India*:

> I saw no reason to waste time. 'I am Ismail Merchant,' I said. 'I am here from America to make films and you will star in them.' [...Shashi] seemed rather taken aback by my approach, but by the end of the evening I had infected him with my enthusiasm.[2]

Ismail Merchant, Jennifer Kendal Kapoor and a pensive Shashi Kapoor (l-r).
Courtesy: Merchant-Ivory Productions.

Shashi confirms: '[Ismail] started attacking me [the moment] he […] entered my house. Anyway, when he came in, there were lots of people […] and they mingled and talked. [But] Mr Merchant was in a hurry to know when he could see me with his director.'[3]

Shashi was two feature films old at that time, having played the lead in *Char Diwari*[4] and *Dharmputra*.[5] He was without the best track record—both movies had fared poorly at the box office. But Ismail—the exuberant, positive, uber salesman that he was known to be—was ready to offer Shashi the world on a platter: 'I said, "Here is an opportunity for you to become an international star. This is a terrific role for you." [Shashi] was completely astonished […] We hit this incredible rapport.'[6]

Once Shashi met both Ismail and James in that tented corridor, he felt compelled to respond to their petitions for *Devgar*. 'I said, this is hardly the place to come to any decision,' Shashi remembers. 'But they wanted a quick decision. And [so] I said, okay, okay, I'll do it.'[7]

Meanwhile, Ismail calls to mind another part of the story— that perhaps Shashi thought that American producers were going to offer him a sizeable remuneration: 'He didn't realize that huge amounts of money were not in the cards.'[8]

As it happened, *Devgar* was never made; the money that Ismail was supposed to raise for the film did not come. But the producer— far from conceding defeat—found another idea to pursue.

On the recommendation of a Hollywood scriptwriter at MGM (Metro–Goldwyn–Mayer), Ismail had read a book written by the German writer, Ruth Prawer Jhabvala, who lived in Delhi with her Indian architect husband. Ismail was riveted by the story of *The Householder*[9] and its ability to capture the nuances of Indian life. He passed on the book to James, who was equally captivated. Straightaway, the two contacted Ruth, who—known for her reluctance to talk to filmmakers—pretended on the phone to be her mother-in-law. Finally, though, the ruse collapsed, and after some hesitation, she agreed to meet them. One can only assume that Ismail and James charmed her with their persuasiveness, for—despite her husband's warning that the duo looked like fly-by-night operators—Ruth not only gave them permission to make a film based on her novel but also agreed to write the script.

Ismail and James, loath to let go of the dream star cast of *Devgar*, decided to involve Shashi, Leela and Durga once more, this time in the new project. But, before they could finalize the actors, Ruth expressed a concern. She thought Shashi was far too handsome to play the role of Prem Sagar, the hapless schoolteacher in *The Householder*. 'If you wanted to make a film about a poor, struggling tutor in some miserable school in Delhi, you probably would not cast someone like Shashi, who was so magnificent,' James tells me. 'He was a grand young man.'

When Shashi heard of Ruth's objections—that he was too glamorous and good looking for the part—he arrived at a rather novel solution. He says, 'I went to a very famous barber shop in Delhi and I said, "I don't want a sophisticated haircut. I want a typical, lower-middle-class Hindi teacher haircut—[for a man] who is very young, very raw. And I want to look like that."'[10]

Subsequently, when Shashi visited Ruth—his thick hair neatly cut, with a staid side parting—and spoke like the character he imagined Prem Sagar to be, Ruth could not help seeing him in a new light. 'So that's how I started [my association] with Merchant–Ivory Productions,' Shashi says.[11]

It didn't take long for Shashi to grow close to James. 'I enjoyed working with Jim [as James was referred to by friends],' he says, 'because he gave me the confidence [...] to do things my way, to use my talent, my intelligence, my sensibilities [to portray] characters in his films.'[12]

James, on his part, says that it was because Shashi was happy to immerse himself in a role, and allow his life experiences,

susceptibilities and inclinations to interact with each part, that he
enjoyed collaborating with the actor: 'Shashi was very easy to work
with. He took direction well. And like any good actor, he sometimes
offered me the choice of doing a scene another way—which I
followed, if it made sense, if it fit in with my idea of the film and if
it wasn't too violent a change in the dialogue. Shashi certainly, and
all actors everywhere, fiddle with the dialogue—they think there is
a slightly better way to say a line, or one word would be better than
another—and I go along with that. Not always, but sometimes, yes.'

1963, *The Householder*. Shashi Kapoor, as Prem Sagar, with a haircut that makes
him seem suitably world-weary, meets the principal, Mr Khanna, played by
the late journalist Romesh Thapar. Courtesy: Merchant-Ivory Productions.

James also feels that Shashi's background in theatre, and the
rigorous years of training under his father, and then his father-in-
law, granted his acting nuance. 'He was completely naturalistic,'
James says. 'There was no overblown style of acting. I have seen

some of his Hindi commercial films, and he really wasn't over-the-top. He had some sense of restraint.' Elsewhere, James adds, 'Shashi had [a] kind of classical training [...] a kind of background that he could draw on as a young actor that most young Indian actors from the Bombay film world don't have. And he also spoke English very well.'[13]

In the meanwhile, in Ismail, Shashi found a lifelong friend, and also a colleague he could at once admire and tease: 'Ismail Merchant, to me, is a hardworking, good producer. I don't think anybody can say that he is a bad producer. But he sometimes acts like a pigeon when he knows that he doesn't have money. [...] You know, when you point a gun at a pigeon [...] the pigeon closes its eyes, thinks that everything will pass away. So Ismail thinks and does things like a pigeon sometimes!' Shashi adds with a playful smile, 'So, when he has no money, he still makes the film. When he has no dates, he still gets the actors to work with him. It's amazing how he continues doing it!'[14]

Ismail, on his part, lightheartedly blames Shashi for his later vices. During the process of editing *The Householder*, it was Shashi who urged a teetotal Ismail to taste his first glass of wine. Ismail writes in his autobiography:

> Even after three years in America I had never drunk wine and Shashi decided it was time I was introduced to the better things in life. 'If you have never tasted wine, then you have wasted your life,' Shashi told me. 'You must have a glass with me.' He corrupted me completely.[15]

Shashi's rapport with Ismail, and his fondness for James, would have a direct bearing on his working relationship with them. They combined their immense talents for seven films made under the Merchant–Ivory Productions banner: *The Householder, Shakespeare Wallah*,[16] *Bombay Talkie*,[17] *Heat and Dust*—all directed by James Ivory—and three films by three other directors—*The Deceivers*,[18] *In Custody*[19] and *Side Streets*.[20]

An amused Shashi Kapoor taking time out with his friend and director, James Ivory,
at the Pulitzer Fountain across the Plaza Hotel in New York City.
Courtesy: Merchant-Ivory Productions.

The Householder (1963)

The Householder was shot in Delhi, mostly in old-world Daryaganj
and the historically rich Mehrauli. When filming began, crowds
thronged the neighbourhoods, waving hysterically and seeking
autographs—Shashi Kapoor's specifically. 'He was already well
known,' James Ivory admits, 'perhaps, in part, because Raj Kapoor
and Shammi Kapoor were his brothers.'

In *The Householder*, Shashi's character, Prem Sagar, has all the
problems of the world on his shoulders—a gorgeous but strong-
willed spouse; an interfering mother who vies with his wife for his
affection; and a poorly-paying job as a Hindi teacher in a school
where he gets no respect from his students, colleagues or the
principal.

Yet, with Ruth Prawer Jhabvala's writing and James' direction,

The Householder, far from getting weighed down by its protagonist's existential crises, turns into a hilarious and charming film. Perhaps, for the first time, Shashi gets to show his comic touch— as in a scene where his wife and he are guests at the school principal's tea party; Leela Naidu (as Indu) fills up her plate and wolfs down the food, while a desperate Prem tries hard to tell her to slow down. (Ironically, the domineering principal—played by the late journalist, Romesh Thapar—has his real-life son, Valmik Thapar, marrying Shashi's real-life daughter, Sanjna Kapoor, many years later.)

1963, *The Householder.* Shashi Kapoor (playing a harried teacher) with his students. Courtesy: Merchant-Ivory Productions.

1963, *The Householder*. Shashi Kapoor with Durga Khote, who plays a nagging, possessive mother. Courtesy: Merchant-Ivory Productions.

1963, *The Householder*. Shashi Kapoor's Prem Sagar with a group of Americans he befriends. 'What kind of yoga do you practise?' an American woman asks a confused Prem. Courtesy: Merchant-Ivory Productions.

1963, *The Householder*. Shashi Kapoor, as the perplexed householder, visits a swami for advice. Courtesy: Merchant-Ivory Productions.

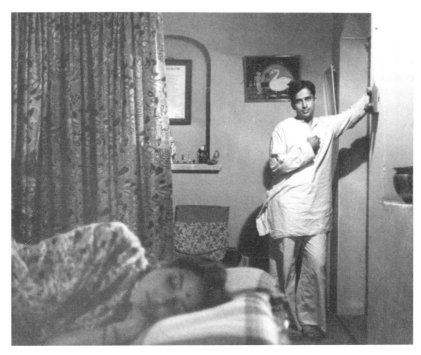

1963, *The Householder*. Shashi Kapoor watches on as the beauteous Leela Naidu, playing his wife, sleeps—a rare moment of tenderness. Courtesy: Merchant-Ivory Productions.

In this scene, and elsewhere, Shashi, despite his attempts at looking dowdy, appears terribly handsome. Leela is, as always, stunningly beautiful, and even Durga Khote's character fascinates as she looks daggers at her daughter-in-law and attacks her with thinly-veiled sarcasm. The trio holds the film aloft with scintillating performances.

However, getting this remarkable movie made was not easy. As always, money was the stumbling block. The film was being shot on a shoestring budget—the little that was raised for *Devgar* was poured into making *The Householder*; James' father, as also Ismail Merchant's, partly funded production costs; and a house that belonged to Ismail's friend was borrowed to capture domestic scenes. But resources soon ran dry. For a while, shooting had to stop completely. Finally, Shashi, who was working for very little money, agreed to defer his fee, as did Ruth. This, along with the timely intervention of a couple of investors, helped *The Householder* teeter to a finish.

If *The Householder* is considered lucky—despite confronting a spate of monetary challenges—it is on account of the unexpected intercession of the legendary filmmaker, Satyajit Ray. James met Satyajit during a visit to Calcutta; it so happened that the Bengali master had seen a short film of his and had liked it. Satyajit introduced James and Ismail to his cinematographer, Subrata Mitra; he loaned them this genius of a cameraman, who went on to shoot *The Householder*, giving it its pristine look with stunning black-and-white montages. In addition, Satyajit stepped in for *The Householder*'s music production—enlisting the help of Ali Akbar Khan, the sitar maestro—and even re-edited the film with his editor, Dulal Dutta, when James and Ismail showed him a rough cut. James recounts how this came to be in an interview with the novelist, Amitav Ghosh:

> After *The Householder* was edited, it still seemed very unwieldy, not very nicely done [...] I asked [Ray] if I

could bring the film to show him. He said sure come on. So Ismail and I climbed on the train—we took the Hindi version of it, all those cans, there must have been twenty-four cans or something. We went from Bombay to Calcutta with all that film. He saw it and liked it—he thought there was something there to work with. I asked him whether he could give us any suggestions about the cutting and he said, yes. He would recut it, but he didn't want me to interfere while he was doing that. He said let me have a go at it, I'll do it my way, you can be in the editing room if you want to be, when we're all done you can change it if you want to, that's your business, but let me do what I want to do. So then he and his editor Dulal Dutt[a] recut the film. They took about four days, and gave it a new shape. It was he [Ray] who suggested that it go into a flashback form.[21]

The Householder was distributed by Columbia Pictures and it opened in October 1963 at the Guild Theater in New York City. While there were a few good reviews, *The New York Times'* Bosley Crowther—considered the ultimate authority on films back then—killed *The Householder*'s box office chances in the city's art-house cinemas. In retrospect, Bosley's review seems rather mean, for it fails to appreciate the independent spirit of the film's production. In language that is especially harsh, even ungenerous, Bosley says this about Shashi:

> Shashi Kapoor, who plays the husband, is colorless and clumsy in what is really a disagreeable role. The stuffy young pedagogue we see here—this peevish aggrandizer of self—doesn't deserve the pretty, amiable and naive little wife that Leela Naidu plays.[22]

After this damning review, Shashi says: '[James] and I went to the Plaza [Hotel]. He used his father's credit card and we plastered

ourselves. [...] We got tight and sentimental and felt sorry for
ourselves.'[23]

That night was all the time Shashi was given to wallow. For,
the next day, the unflappable Ismail and the resilient James were
chasing yet another movie dream, and roping in the dejected
actor.

James Ivory, Leela Naidu, Shashi Kapoor, Ismail Merchant (l-r) at the premiere of
The Householder. Courtesy: Merchant-Ivory Productions.

Shakespeare Wallah (1965)

James Ivory had been toying with the idea of a film that followed a
group of travelling Indian actors putting up modern Indian English
plays across cities. But Ruth Prawer Jhabvala thought there was
something unrealistic about this proposal. James says, 'Ruth said
that the kind of people who'd want to be part of high-flown
English plays would not take up the lives of itinerant actors.
They'd abhor that idea. She said it was a fake notion.'

But it was this 'unrealistic' idea that led James to the Shakespeareana team—the group of British travelling actors led by Geoffrey and Laura Liddell Kendal. Already, he had met the Kendals socially while shooting *The Householder*, since Jennifer Kendal Kapoor had been spending considerable time in Delhi with her husband. Now, he chose to acquaint himself more intimately with the theatre troupe, and took Ruth along with him.

Drawing extensively from the diaries of Geoffrey, *Shakespeare Wallah* is Chekhovian in its content and style. It projects the desolate lives of travelling British actors who desperately try to keep Shakespeare alive in an independent, fast-changing India— an India where audiences would rather invest in popular, lowbrow cinema and cheery movie stars than engage with solemn plays and struggling actors.

While the Kendals appear in the film as fictionalized versions of themselves—Geoffrey is cast as the troupe leader, Tony Buckingham, and Laura, as his wife and partner, Carla—Geoffrey was not thrilled with the script or the upshot. 'The film was not about us,' Geoffrey writes in his autobiography '[It] concerned some travelling showmen to whom we bore no resemblance.'[24] Despite this, Geoffrey did not hesitate to borrow the title of James' film for his book. And years later, he finally conceded that he appreciated the spirit of the film—'it deserves the praise and fame it has earned.'[25]

Shashi Kapoor was cast in *Shakespeare Wallah* as a shallow but wealthy playboy, Sanju, who flirts not only with a Hindi movie starlet, but also a British actress from the theatre troupe, Lizzie— played by Jennifer's sister, Felicity Kendal, who was seventeen at that time and had been contracted to act for seventy-five rupees. Shashi found acting alongside his sister-in-law nothing short of a revelation. He says, 'Because I had toured with Shakespearana, I had been in close contact with the family. Even after marriage, Felicity Kendal was very close to my wife and me. I knew her, but

I had no idea that [this girl with no experience in the movies] would be so good. [...] She would totally get involved in the character and forget her real self. [...] Felicity Kendal was stealing the show. It was her film.'[26]

The 'sudden, electric and brief'[27] romance between Sanju and Lizzie in *Shakespeare Wallah,* and the unspooling of their relationship—these scenes carry within them a great deal of poignancy. But for followers of family-trees and bisecting relationships, *Shakespeare Wallah* is also memorable for the delicate kiss Sanju shares with Lizzie—or Shashi shares with his sister-in-law. Summoning up that moment, Shashi says, 'I think it was the first film [in which] I ever kissed [...] It was a bit embarrassing for me and I realized that it would be very embarrassing for Felicity.'[28]

A central character in *Shakespeare Wallah* is Manjula—the sassy, glamourous Hindi movie starlet dallying with Sanju—for which part James and Ismail cast their New York-based theatre actress friend, Madhur Jaffrey. James and Ismail had been introduced to each other through Madhur's late husband and actor, Saeed Jaffrey (the two would divorce), and later, Madhur became a regular member of the Merchant–Ivory team, performing in three more productions directed by James—*The Guru,*[29] *Autobiography of a Princess,*[30] *Heat and Dust*—and also, in *The Perfect Murder*[31] (for which Ismail was executive producer) and *Cotton Mary,*[32] which she co-directed with Ismail.

For Madhur, being part of *Shakespeare Wallah* was exhilarating for many reasons, but also because she'd be working with Shashi for the first time—who, by then, had become a prominent star in the Hindi film galaxy. 'Of course, I knew Shashi from his films—Hindi cinema,' Madhur says. 'I always thought Shashi was one of the best looking men. And the idea of acting with him was very exciting. Then, I met him for the first time. And he was happy—a positive, young man—and greeted me very nicely. And I thought, this was going to be all right.'

Madhur's Manjula, as Lizzie's rival, has some of the strongest scenes in *Shakespeare Wallah* as she testily demands Sanju's attention. It is a performance that Shashi provides the perfect foil for. 'The scenes that I had with Shashi were intimate,' Madhur says. 'They were two people who were lovers. I was doing my first film, and Shashi was clear that acting was all fun—just don't take it too seriously—that was the kind of attitude he had, especially in a tense situation when I wasn't used to being in front of a film crew.'

As was the case with *The Householder*, *Shakespeare Wallah* was made on a tight budget. Once more, Ruth and Shashi agreed to defer their salaries—it was only in 1970 that Ismail eventually settled the money he owed Shashi when he produced *Bombay Talkie*.

In another uncanny resemblance with *The Householder*, Satyajit Ray was a presence for *Shakespeare Wallah*, too—with his cinematographer, Subrata Mitra, shooting the film and Satyajit composing the original score. Years later, in 2007, American film director, Wes Anderson, would use many of the musical pieces from *Shakespeare Wallah* for his India-based dramedy, *The Darjeeling Limited*.[33]

Shakespeare Wallah played in the competition section of the 15th Berlin International Film Festival, partly on the recommendation of Satyajit, whose *Charulata*[34]—considered a masterpiece by many—was also in the running. While Madhur won the Silver Bear for best actress, Satyajit won the Silver Bear for best director for *Charulata*, making 1965 a remarkably good year for India in Germany.

It was in Berlin that Madhur and Shashi found themselves in the middle of an amusing mix-up. The two actors were in the elevator at Hotel Amzo when they realized that the Italian actress, Gina Lollobrigida, was also sharing the lift with them. Introductions were made, and Gina, who was known as a sex symbol, was obviously drawn to Shashi's good looks. Madhur tells me, 'The next day, a huge, most beautiful bunch of flowers arrived for me in my room, saying, "Will you have lunch with me?" with Gina's signature. And I looked at the bouquet and I knew that there had been a mistake. How could Gina possibly distinguish between the names, Shashi Kapoor and Madhur Jaffrey—who is a man and who is a woman from the Italian point of view? She must have thought I was Shashi. I remember going to Shashi's room, plonking the flowers in front of him and saying, "Shashi, I know these are for you. But if you want me to go have lunch with her, I will."'

Ismail remembers more about the incident. In his autobiography, he writes:

> It wasn't until the last night of our visit, at a party given by the festival, that a very vexed Gina—whose advances, presumably, were rarely spurned—made a point of confronting Shashi, and discovered her mistake. Poor Shashi was terribly disappointed that the confusion had caused him to miss such an opportunity.[35]

Shakespeare Wallah went on to play at the New York and London Film Festivals. And Shashi's performance was appreciated by many. *Variety*'s unnamed critic, while applauding the film's 'naive charm', adds: 'There is also a very confident performance by Shashi Kapoor, as the Indian playboy.'[36] *Life* magazine's Richard Schickel, fulsome in his praise for the film's 'humanity, its intelligence and its imagery', says that 'Ivory and his scriptwriter, R. Prawer Jhabwala [*sic*], are wonderfully served by their actors.'[37] Even Bosley Crowther of *The New York Times* is (relatively) kind to *Shakespeare Wallah*:

> Within the telling of this story [of the struggles and the last days of the travelling British theatre group], Mr. Ivory

and his almost perfect cast [...] have managed to convey a countless number of strong implications and subtle hints that quiver with irony, sadness and benign resignation to change.[38]

Crowther's review eventually helped *Shakespeare Wallah* earn an eight-week run at the Baronet & Coronet—an art-house theatre on the East Side of Manhattan.

But the most perceptive comment came from Shashi's father-in-law, Geoffrey Kendal, who in a letter to his daughter, Felicity, writes: 'He [Shashi] should go into films in English with foreign directors who know how to exploit him.'[39]

Bombay Talkie (1970)

For their fourth film set in India (James Ivory directed *The Guru* in the interval in 1969), Merchant–Ivory Productions decided to focus on Bombay's flamboyant Hindi film industry. It was Ruth Prawer Jhabvala's idea—a story about a British bestselling writer seeking fodder from 'Bollywood' for her next big book, while journeying through the star-system of Indian filmdom. Ismail Merchant, always a big fan of Hindi cinema—his favourite star was the 1950s actress, Nimmi—loved the fact that the film would get to show the kitschy, garish elements of tinsel-town. *Bombay Talkie* was the obvious choice of title, and once more, Subrata Mitra was the cinematographer.

Shashi Kapoor, but naturally, was selected to act as the big film star, Vikram, who would fall in love with the writer, Lucia Lane, played by his real-life wife, Jennifer Kendal Kapoor. In what would be one of the few negative roles he would portray in his career, a self-absorbed Vikram cheats on his young wife, Mala (played by Aparna Sen), and wrests the attention of Lucia from his friend, Hari, a quiet scriptwriter (played by the Pakistani actor, Zia Mohyeddin).

However, before Shashi could commit to *Bombay Talkie,* there was the uncomfortable question of the money he had been promised for *The Householder* and *Shakespeare Wallah.* While Shashi considered Ismail a close friend, he wanted to clear past financial dues. But, as would be a regular affair with Ismail, he was short of funds once again. Finally, it was Jennifer who came to his rescue. Ismail writes:

> Jennifer always had a soft spot for me. [She] lent me the money to pay Shashi. So, in effect, I used Shashi's own money to settle my debt with him. Of course I returned the money to Jennifer as soon as I was able to, but the whole transaction remained a secret with Shashi.[40]

And that is how *Bombay Talkie* found its star. James Ivory says, '*Bombay Talkie* was a really enjoyable film to make with Shashi

1970, *Bombay Talkie.* An oft-discussed scene, where Shashi Kapoor shares a kiss with his wife, Jennifer Kendal. Courtesy: Merchant-Ivory Productions.

and Jennifer playing lovers. The whole film was—well, no film is easy—but it was enjoyable and Shashi liked doing it. He was pretty pleased.'

While Aparna's role in the film is small—she refers to it as the 'least interesting' of her collaborations with Shashi, which include him being the producer of her first directorial venture, *36 Chowringhee Lane*[41]—she had a chance to observe James, Subrata and Shashi closely on the sets. She says, 'I remember, once, during *Bombay Talkie*, Subrata was taking very long to set up—the whole room was full of mirrors, and he didn't know where to hide his lights. Finally, when Subrata said he was ready, Shashi said he was not in a mood to act! Shashi may have been a known actor back then, but Subrata was the bigger star of the two. However, Shashi had been sitting there for a long time, and was annoyed.

'Suddenly, in the middle of this tiff, Jim [James Ivory] started pulling his nose. It became red. And he began grinning. In fact, each time something unpleasant happened, Jim's first reaction was not to lose his cool, but to laugh. He was like a child. So, he beamed and asked Shashi, "When do you think you will be in the right mood?" And Shashi said, "I don't know, after half an hour!" Then, quietly, he came back and shot the scene.'

This wasn't the only occasion when James had to firefight with a smile. 'I had a kissing scene with Shashi,' Aparna tells me. 'And I was most upset because I hadn't been informed earlier—I was told on the set! Jim grinned and said, yes, you have to do it. And along with Shashi, he kept teasing me. I had to give in. It was the first time I kissed on screen.'

While *Bombay Talkie* opened to mixed reviews—the *New York Times* called it James' 'most ambitious' film, and then, 'in American terms, [the] least successful'[42]—it is remembered for its sumptuous rendering of the Indian 'dream factory', and its opening Busby Berkeley-inspired dance number on a giant typewriter; Helen and

Shashi jumping on the keys, as Kishore Kumar sings a wonderfully delirious song, 'Typewriter Tip Tip Tip Tip Karta Hai, Zindagi Ki Har Kahani Likhta Hai'.[43] It is a sequence that outdoes 'Bollywood' pop-extravagance!

Bombay Talkie could well have been known as the first of many films starring Shashi and his friend, Amitabh Bachchan—but this piece of cinematic history was not meant to be. According to James, Amitabh was supposed to play the role of a struggling actor in a scene where the veteran character actress, Nadira, is surrounded by male admirers. But Amitabh did not show up! 'For some reason,' James says, 'he withdrew from the part. But the problem was, we had already shot him in one scene—where Shashi's body is being cremated and several young men are part of the crowd

1970, *Bombay Talkie*. Shashi Kapoor's third Merchant-Ivory film hits the giant screens.
Courtesy: Merchant-Ivory Productions.

1970, *Bombay Talkie*. The opening scene where Shashi Kapoor's Vikram dances on a giant typewriter-set with Helen, as Kishore Kumar and Asha Bhosle sing, 'Typewriter Tip Tip Tip Tip Karta Hai'. Courtesy: Merchant–Ivory Productions.

around the funeral pyre—Amitabh was in that frame. Finally, we cut it off the film.'

Shashi explains the mysterious disappearance of Amitabh, while describing a scene in *Bombay Talkie* where Jennifer's car is stopped on the road for the funeral procession. 'Amitabh was one of the actors in the crowd of men,' he says. 'I told him to leave the set and not do the role. He was upset, saying he would lose out on earning Rs 50.'[44]

Amitabh, in turn, corroborates this. 'Yes, the story of *Bombay Talkie* is correct.' Then, he adds, 'Shashi said: "Don't do these bit parts. You are made for better things."'

Shashi's words—which, back then, had 'annoyed'[45] a struggling Amitabh, who had just arrived in Bombay and was not getting any work—would prove prophetic.

Heat and Dust (1983)

Shashi Kapoor's fourth and last film with James Ivory as director was *Heat and Dust*, based on Ruth Prawer Jhabvala's 1975 Booker Prize-winning novel of the same name. It would also be the first grand scale production that the Merchant–Ivory team would become known for with future Oscar-winning films like *A Room with a View*[46] and *Howards End*.[47]

Heat and Dust has an impressive star cast, with Julie Christie playing a modern-day English woman, Ann, in search of an India that her grand-aunt had come into contact with in 1920. Greta Scacchi—who was only twenty-three at the time of the film's release and performing on screen for the first time—was cast as Olivia, Ann's aunt and also the wife of a British civil servant in India; Olivia would end up having an affair with a local nawab.

Naturally, Shashi was cast as the nawab. He was forty-five at the time of the film's release, regal in appearance and at the peak of his career in Hindi cinema, having completed *Shaan*,[48] *Kalyug*,[49] *Namak Halaal*[50] and *Vijeta*.[51] 'He was twenty years older than when he had made *The Householder*,' James says. 'He looked mature and as handsome as ever. My goodness, he made the perfect nawab.' In another interview, James adds: 'Shashi always played princes in our movies—except in *The Householder*. He plays a rich playboy in *Shakespeare Wallah*. And then, when we did *Bombay Talkie*, he's a movie star at the height of his looks and career. And then, when we go on to *Heat and Dust*, he is a nawab. He was really put on this earth to play these kinds of parts.'[52]

Madhur Jaffrey, who had acted as one of Shashi's love interests in *Shakespeare Wallah*, read the script of *Heat and Dust* and was keen, this time around, to play his mother, the begum. Since the actress is only five years older than Shashi, James was convinced that the casting would not work. As Madhur recalls, 'I don't know who he had in his mind, but he said to me, "I can't have you play the begum because that would be so ungallant of me."' Finally, won over by Madhur's persuasion, James changed his mind.

As would happen often with Merchant–Ivory productions, financiers suddenly pulled out and with that, funds for the film dried up. Three weeks into the shoot in Hyderabad, there was no money to pay the actors and the crew; worse, when the team was ready to move to the next location, the hotel bills had to be settled. Ismail Merchant, who was already in Kashmir, asked Shashi to be the guarantor for the bills. While James says, 'I was kept away from these kinds of details,' he does confirm that Shashi bailed them out.

Despite a spate of financial crises, *Heat and Dust* did get made, and it was a hit. Along with Richard Attenborough's *Gandhi*,[53] which had swept the Oscars the year before, and the success of two television series set in British India—*The Jewel and the Crown*[54] and *The Far Pavilions*[55]—*Heat and Dust* placed the country firmly on the international map; India became the flavour of the times.

As a student at Columbia University's journalism school, I remember seeing *Heat and Dust* in its opening weekend at Paris

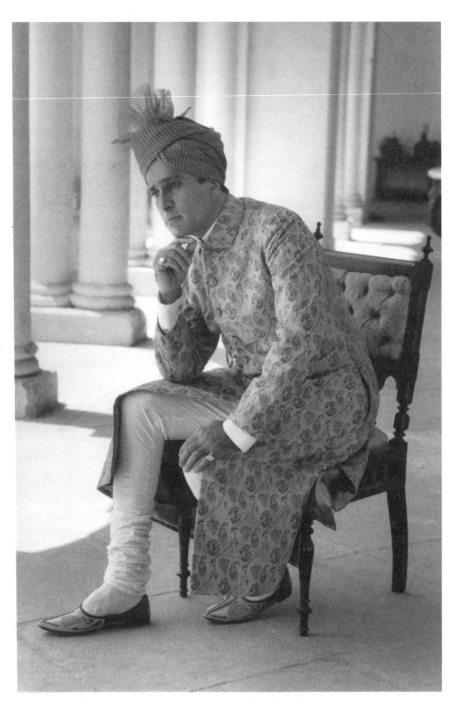

1983, *Heat and Dust.* Shashi Kapoor as the nawab. Courtesy: Merchant-Ivory Productions.

1983, *Heat and Dust*. 'Shashi Kapoor was put on this earth to play the prince': James Ivory.
Courtesy: Merchant-Ivory Productions.

Theatre in midtown Manhattan. The ticket holders' line snaked around the block, and when we finally seated ourselves in the semi-dark hall, I couldn't help feeling exhilarated that India and a majestic Shashi were on a giant screen in New York City.

While Shashi had travelled abroad for *Shakespeare Wallah*, it was with *Heat and Dust* that he got to savour the full experience of being an American celebrity. Shashi says:

> I went to a Universal Studio tour. It was full of posters of *Heat and Dust*. Shashi Kapoor was everywhere [...] The airlines lost my clothes and I had a new suit made in hours for the reception at the Plaza [in New York City] given by the legendary Harry Winston. Placido Domingo was there.[56]

That opening night, the *Heat and Dust* team stayed awake to catch the first of the reviews in the morning newspapers—all of which were positive. Later, in the *Chicago Sun-Times*, Roger Ebert refers to Shashi's nawab as 'beguiling, attractive, cheerfully sophisticated.'[57] And in *The New York Times*, Vincent Canby, while applauding the entire team—'of all their collaborations, none has been more graceful, funny, literate or entertaining than *Heat and Dust*'—goes on to acknowledge the complexity of Shashi's role: 'Mr Kapoor [...] is both funny and mysterious as the nawab, whose perfect manners may be the mask of either a fool or a villain.'[58] Shashi had travelled a long way.

Siddhartha (1972)

Conrad Rooks, a New Yorker and the son of the founding president of Avon, was deeply inspired by Hermann Hesse's 1922 novel[59] and its protagonist, Siddhartha—a restless boy, who travels long and far in pursuit of the true meaning of life. Along the way, Siddhartha encounters the Buddha, whose teachings he appreciates but cannot imbibe; a stunning courtesan, Kamala, who (temporarily) makes him reassess his destiny; and a ferryman, who reminds him that each spiritual quest is unique, and that while knowledge can be taught, wisdom must be drawn from experience.

Siddhartha and Conrad were, in some ways, similar—both were hippies in India on a journey of self-discovery. But while Siddhartha experienced a flash of spiritual illumination by a river, Conrad had his moment of epiphany at Raj Kapoor's studio, and it led him down a road that wasn't exactly 'spiritual':

> So I [...was at Raj Kapoor's] small office. And he was sitting like a pasha on a platform and the servant kept coming in bringing him scotch and soda. And in the meantime, all these distributors showed up and they were begging him to finish this movie that was [being shot] outside, and they were also bringing him trunks of money, suitcases of money. And so I thought to myself, this is the thing for me, this is the life for me. I have to get into the movie business [...] I can live like a maharaja in India![60]

We'll never know if Conrad's far-fetched claims are true, but what we do know is that he decided to make a film based on Hermann's novel, and arrived at a list of actors. While he was advised to sign on Peter Fonda for the lead role, the director wished to have an Indian star cast, and could not think of anyone better suited to play the hero than Shashi—he had met the actor with Jennifer Kendal Kapoor at Hotel Sun-n-Sand in Juhu during an earlier visit to Bombay. Simi Garewal, who had by then acted in a range of art-house and commercial films—from Satyajit Ray's *Aranyer Din Ratri*[61] to Raj Kapoor's *Mera Naam Joker*[62]—was cast as the exquisite Kamala.

Conrad spared no cost, using part of his sizeable inheritance from his father to fund *Siddhartha*. He hired Ingmar Bergman's regular cameraman (often referred to as Bergman's 'eyes'), Sven Nykvist, who brought a Swedish team with him, to capture the

chaotic beauty of North India, and the quasi-mystical
neighbourhoods of Haridwar and Rishikesh. He enlisted British
and American crew members. For music, he hired the talent of
Hemant Kumar, who in addition to composing the score, also
used two of his hit Bengali songs from older films—'O Nodi Re'[63]
and 'Pather Klanti Bhule'.[64]

What Conrad didn't bargain for was the Indo–Pakistani War
in December 1971, which delayed the shooting of the film. For a
tense fortnight, the *Siddhartha* team remained holed up in Delhi's
Oberoi Maidens Hotel. Uneasy about what was to follow, some of
the British crew left. David McKibben, who was hired by Conrad
as a location scout and production manager, remembers the
dilemma the production team was in. 'We were about to move
forward, but now we had no production or sound people!'

At this point, Shashi found himself not only cobbling together
a team with Conrad, but also attempting to rehearse his lines such
that his delivery met with the director's approval. Simi remembers
these practice sessions with Shashi. She says, 'I prefer "natural"
acting, but Conrad specifically wanted us to be "classic stylized" in
our performance since it was a period film and not modern.'

After supervising gruelling rehearsals during times of war,
Conrad faced yet another dilemma—Shashi was famous, and it
was impossible to shoot on the frenzied roads of Rishikesh. A
substantial part of the shoot, consequently, had to be in the estate
of the maharaja of Bharatpur, where entry was restricted. It proved
to be a good decision. 'There was a kind of timelessness throughout
the shoot,' Simi tells me. 'No rush. Nothing frantic. It was smooth,
like the tranquillity of the film.'

Then came the time to shoot the intimate scenes between
Siddhartha and Kamala—for which Conrad was inspired by the
sculptures of Konark and Khajuraho. 'There wasn't a lot of sex,'
David is quick to clarify. 'It was suggestive and tastefully done.'
But the scenes did require kissing and Simi had to be shot partially

in the nude. 'I can't tell you how nervous I was before these scenes,' Simi says. 'The Swedish crew couldn't understand my anxiety. Sven told me, "In Sweden, when we set up a nude sequence, the actors just remove their clothes and sit around waiting!" I finally wore a body-stocking from the waist down, but when I had to go topless, I was stricken. I couldn't look up and just lowered my eyes. Shashi sensed what I was going through and said to me, "Don't be shy, Simi. You are beautiful." Buoyed by his words, I found the courage to go through it all with confidence.'

It was an extremely patient Shashi who also taught Simi how to kiss for the camera. 'Since he had performed love scenes in Hollywood films, Shashi explained to me how one should keep the angle of one's face for a screen kiss,' she says. 'Also, he added, "Limited pressure, so it doesn't distort the face."'

I first saw *Siddhartha* in a small art-house theatre in London in 1974, two years before it opened in India. I was moved by the film's pace, the numinous locations and the tender moments between Siddhartha and Kamala. But most of all, I remember being mesmerized by Hemant's voice, and stepping out of the theatre humming 'O Nodi Re' on the streets of London—a tune that Hemant would later use for 'O Bekarar Dil'[65] in *Kohraa*.[66]

Siddhartha released in India in 1976—but not before battling controversies, mostly revolving around the nude scenes. The press went to town, with one magazine leaking advance images of a topless Simi with Shashi; Simi sued. In the midst of such sound and fury, the film, quite incredibly, survived the Indian censors, who passed *Siddhartha* with minor cuts. Conrad Rooks got to brag: 'I ended up showing the first lovemaking scene in Indian cinema and the first kiss on the screen or series of kisses.'[67] As always, his claims were somewhat exaggerated; Indian cinema's first ever on-screen kiss had been filmed four decades earlier, in the 1933 movie, *Karma*.[68]

Siddhartha was not well received. Critics were quick to condemn

Shashi's stylized acting and stilted dialogue delivery, and panned
the film as a whole—*Variety*'s unnamed critic denounced
Siddhartha's 'surface elegance which sometimes robs the film of its
needed earthiness';[69] *The New York Times*' Vincent Canby dismissed
it as 'a small-scale *Ten Commandments* for flower children';[70] and
the *Chicago Sun Times*' Roger Ebert summed up the flaws that
marred the film:

> The trouble is that the movie's almost too pretty. We get
> sunsets and vistas and slow-moving rivers and dust in the
> sunlight and magnificent Indian settings (man-made and
> real). And against all of this splendor, the activities of the
> characters seem somehow unreal and not crucial. It's as if
> the people in the movie always thought of themselves in
> silhouette and back-lit. As a general rule, characters
> shouldn't act as if they know they're in a movie. It distracts
> us, and it distracts them.[71]

Interestingly, the audiences in America, and especially on college
campuses—traumatized as they were by the Vietnam War and the
aftermath of the civil rights movement—took a liking to this film
that spoke of angst and individualism. *Siddhartha*, while never a
box office success, became a cult classic. It toured the world.

Simi and Shashi went to New York for the film's premiere, and
in September 1972, accompanied Conrad for the Venice Film
Festival. 'The *Siddhartha* night will remain with me as long as I
live,' Simi says. 'Shashi and I walked from Hotel Excelsior to the
theatre. Shashi, in a dark Jodhpur, looked exquisite beside me. I
had on my *Siddhartha* head jewellery and wore a long train on my
evening coat, and some young Italian boys picked up the edges
and trailed behind me all the way. The paparazzi went mad!' After
the screening, there was a round of applause that lasted a whole
fifteen minutes. 'It was magical, surreal,' Simi says. *Siddhartha*
went on to win the Silver Lion Award in Venice.

1972, *Siddhartha*. Shashi Kapoor playing the reluctant hermit, and a beautiful Simi Garewal as a courtesan. Courtesy: Alexander Rooks/Lotus Films.

1972, *Siddhartha*. A film that will be mired in controversy. In this scene, Kamala teaches Siddhartha how to kiss. In reality, it was Shashi Kapoor who taught Simi Garewal how to kiss for the camera. Courtesy: Alexander Rooks/Lotus Films.

On their last night in Italy, Shashi and Simi went on a gondola ride. The gondolier sang and, quite unexpectedly, Shashi leapt up. 'Our mild, ever-dignified, always-so-proper Shashi started a peculiar half-Hindi duet with the gondolier!' Simi tells me. 'Each Italian verse was followed by a made-up Hindi line. He was so funny, I couldn't stop laughing. Then Shashi started singing some Shammi Kapoor numbers with abandon on top of his voice! Now, Shashi *can't* sing! But passing gondoliers cheered and clapped. It was like a comic scene from a film.'

It is this that I have come to appreciate as I talk to Shashi's closest friends, his associates and co-stars—the lightness of touch that Shashi brings, not just to his films, but to life. No matter the gravitas of his characters, or the sobriety of his performances, or how his films are perceived by critics and audiences, Shashi, in essence, is an actor and a man who refuses to be burdened by solemnity.

Notes

1. Robert Emmet Long, *James Ivory in Conversation* (Los Angeles, University of California Press, 2005), p. 67.
2. Ismail Merchant, *My Passage from India: A Filmmaker's Journey from Bombay to Hollywood* (New York: Viking Studio, 2002), p. 43.
3. Based on an interview with Shashi Kapoor in the Criterion Collection DVD of the 1963 film, *The Householder*, dir. James Ivory, prod. Ismail Merchant, starring Shashi Kapoor, Leela Naidu, Durga Khote.
4. 1961, *Char Diwari*, dir. Krishan Chopra, prod. Jagan Prasad Sharma, starring Shashi Kapoor, Nanda, Manmohan Krishna.
5. 1961, *Dharmputra*, dir. Yash Chopra, prod. B.R. Chopra, starring Shashi Kapoor, Mala Sinha, Rehman.
6. Based on an interview with Ismail Merchant in the Criterion Collection DVD of *The Householder*.
7. Based on an interview with Shashi Kapoor in the Criterion Collection DVD of *The Householder*.
8. Based on an interview with Ismail Merchant in the Criterion Collection DVD of *The Householder*.

9. Ruth Prawer Jhabvala, *The Householder* (New York: W.W. Norton & Company, 1960).
10. Based on an interview with Shashi Kapoor in the Criterion Collection DVD of *The Householder*.
11. *Ibid.*
12. *Ibid.*
13. Based on an interview with James Ivory in the Criterion Collection DVD of the 1983 film, *Heat and Dust*, dir. James Ivory, prod. Ismail Merchant, starring Julie Christie, Greta Scacchi, Shashi Kapoor.
14. Based on an interview with Shashi Kapoor in the Criterion Collection DVD of *Heat and Dust*.
15. Ismail Merchant, *My Passage from India: A Filmmaker's Journey from Bombay to Hollywood* (New York: Viking Studio, 2002), p. 50.
16. 1965, *Shakespeare Wallah*, dir. James Ivory, prod. Ismail Merchant, starring Shashi Kapoor, Felicity Kendal, Madhur Jaffrey.
17. 1970, *Bombay Talkie*, dir. James Ivory, prod. Ismail Merchant, starring Shashi Kapoor, Jennifer Kendal, Zia Mohyeddin.
18. 1988, *The Deceivers*, dir. Nicholas Meyer, prod. Ismail Merchant, starring Pierce Brosnan, Shashi Kapoor, Saeed Jaffrey.
19. 1993, *In Custody*, dir. Ismail Merchant, prod. Wahid Chowhan, starring Shashi Kapoor, Shabana Azmi, Om Puri.
20. 1998, *Side Streets*, dir. Tony Gerber, prod. Bruce Weiss, starring Valeria Golino, Shashi Kapoor, Shabana Azmi.
21. Amitav Ghosh, 'Satyajit Ray', *Outlook*, 22 June 2004.
22. Bosley Crowther, 'The Householder: Movie Review', *The New York Times*, 22 October 1963.
23. Quoted in Madhu Jain, *The Kapoors: The First Family of Indian Cinema* (New Delhi: Penguin, 2005), p. 238.
24. Geoffrey Kendal, *The Shakespeare Wallah: An Autobiography* (London: Sidgwick & Jackson, 1986), p. 145.
25. *Ibid.*, p. 154.
26. Based on an interview with Shashi Kapoor in the Criterion Collection DVD of *Shakespeare Wallah*.
27. Bosley Crowther, 'Shakespeare Wallah: Movie Review', *The New York Times*, 23 March 1966.
28. Based on an interview with Shashi Kapoor in the Criterion Collection DVD of *Shakespeare Wallah*.
29. 1969, *The Guru*, dir. James Ivory, prod. Ismail Merchant, starring Michael York, Madhur Jaffrey, Zohra Sehgal.
30. 1975, *Autobiography of a Princess*, dir. James Ivory, prod. Ismail Merchant, starring James Mason, Madhur Jaffrey, Diane Fletcher.

31. 1988, *The Perfect Murder*, dir. Zafar Hai, prod. Wahid Chowhan, starring Naseeruddin Shah, Madhur Jaffrey, Ratna Pathak.
32. 1999, *Cotton Mary*, dir. Ismail Merchant, prod. Nayeem Hafizka, Richard Hawley, starring Greta Scacchi, Madhur Jaffrey, James Wilby.
33. 2007, *The Darjeeling Limited*, dir. Wes Anderson, prod. Wes Anderson, Roman Coppola, Lydia Dean Pilcher, Scott Rudin, starring Owen Wilson, Adrien Brody, Jason Schwartzman.
34. 1964, *Charulata*, dir. Satyajit Ray, prod. R.D. Bansal, starring Soumitra Chatterjee, Madhabi Mukherjee, Sailen Mukherjee.
35. Ismail Merchant, *My Passage from India: A Filmmaker's Journey from Bombay to Hollywood* (New York: Viking Studio, 2002), p. 63.
36. 'Review: Shakespeare Wallah', *Variety*, 31 December 1964.
37. Richard Schickel, 'A Sweet and Subtle Idyl in India: Shakespeare Wallah', *Life*, 19 April 1966.
38. Bosley Crowther, 'Shakespeare Wallah: Movie Review', *The New York Times*, 23 March 1966.
39. Geoffrey Kendal in a letter to Felicity Kendal, dated 30 July 1965. Felicity Kendal, *White Cargo* (London: Michael Joseph, 1998), p. 207.
40. Ismail Merchant, *My Passage from India: A Filmmaker's Journey from Bombay to Hollywood* (New York: Viking Studio, 2002), p. 73.
41. 1981, *36 Chowringhee Lane*, dir. Aparna Sen, prod. Shashi Kapoor, starring Jennifer Kendal, Debashree Roy, Dhritiman Chatterjee.
42. Vincent Canby, 'Bombay Talkie: Movie Review', *The New York Times*, 19 November 1970.
43. 'Typewriter Tip Tip Tip Tip Karta Hai', lyr. Hasrat Jaipuri, comp. Shankar–Jaikishan, artists Asha Bhosle, Kishore Kumar.
44. Quoted in Jessica Hines, *Looking for the Big B: Bollywood, Bachchan and Me* (London: Bloomsbury, 2007), p. 101.
45. *Ibid.*, p. 102.
46. 1985, *A Room with a View*, dir. James Ivory, prod. Ismail Merchant, starring Maggie Smith, Helena Bonham Carter, Denholm Elliott.
47. 1992, *Howards End*, dir. James Ivory, prod. Ismail Merchant, starring Anthony Hopkins, Vanessa Redgrave, Helena Bonham Carter.
48. 1980, *Shaan*, dir. Ramesh Sippy, prod. G.P. Sippy, starring Sunil Dutt, Amitabh Bachchan, Shashi Kapoor, Raakhee, Parveen Babi.
49. 1981, *Kalyug*, dir. Shyam Benegal, prod. Shashi Kapoor, starring Shashi Kapoor, Rekha, Raj Babbar.
50. 1982, *Namak Halaal*, dir. Prakash Mehra, prod. Satyendra Pal, starring Amitabh Bachchan, Shashi Kapoor, Smita Patil, Waheeda Rehman, Parveen Babi.

51. 1982, *Vijeta*, dir. Govind Nihalani, prod. Shashi Kapoor, starring Shashi Kapoor, Rekha, Kunal Kapoor.
52. Based on an interview with James Ivory in the Criterion Collection DVD of *Heat and Dust*.
53. 1982, *Gandhi*, dir. Richard Attenborough, prod. Richard Attenborough, starring Ben Kingsley, Rohini Hattangadi, Roshan Seth.
54. 1984, *The Jewel in the Crown* [TV series], dir. Jim O' Brien, Christopher Morahan, prod. Christopher Morahan, starring Art Malik, Saeed Jaffrey, Peggy Ashcroft.
55. 1984, *The Far Pavilions* [TV series], dir. Peter Duffell, prod. Geoffrey Reeve, starring Ben Cross, Amy Irving, Christopher Lee.
56. Quoted in Madhu Jain, *The Kapoors: The First Family of Indian Cinema* (New Delhi: Penguin, 2005), p. 244.
57. Roger Ebert, 'Heat and Dust', *Chicago Sun-Times*, 20 October 1983.
58. Vincent Cranby, 'Heat and Dust: Movie Review', *The New York Times*, 15 September 1983.
59. Hermann Hesse, *Siddhartha*, translated by Hilda Rosner (New Delhi: Rupa, 2010).
60. Based on an interview in the DVD of the 1972 film, *Siddhartha*, dir. Conrad Rooks, prod. Conrad Rooks, starring Shashi Kapoor, Simi Garewal, Romesh Sharma.
61. 1970, *Aranyer Din Ratri*, dir. Satyajit Ray, prod. Asim Dutta, Nepal Dutta, starring Soumitra Chatterjee, Sharmila Tagore, Simi Garewal.
62. 1970, *Mera Naam Joker*, dir. Raj Kapoor, prod. Raj Kapoor, starring Raj Kapoor, Simi Garewal, Manoj Kumar.
63. 'O Nodi Re', lyr. Gouri Prasanna Majumdar, comp. Hemant Kumar, artist Hemant Kumar.
64. 'Pather Klanti Bhule', lyr. Gouri Prasanna Majumdar, comp. Hemant Kumar, artist Hemant Kumar.
65. 'O Bekarar Dil', lyr. Kaifi Azmi, comp. Hemant Kumar, artist Lata Mangeshkar.
66. 1964, *Kohraa*, dir. Biren Nag, prod. Hemant Kumar, starring Biswajeet, Waheeda Rehman, Lalita Pawar.
67. Based on an interview with Conrad Rooks in the DVD of *Siddhartha*.
68. 1933, *Karma*, dir. J.L. Freer Hunt, prod. Himanshu Rai, starring Devika Rani, Himanshu Rai, Abraham Sofaer.
69. 'Review: Siddhartha', *Variety*, 31 December 1971.
70. Vincent Canby, 'Siddhartha: Movie Review', *The New York Times*, 19 July 1973.
71. Roger Ebert, 'Siddhartha', *Chicago Sun-Times*, 18 July 1973.

4

THE TAXI
Shashi and the Madding 1970s

'My father-in-law used to call Shashi Uncle "taxi" back then,' Neetu Singh Kapoor says. '*Ki kisi ko bhi apni gaadi main bitha leta hai!*' ('He'd seat anyone and everyone in his car.')

Neetu speaks figuratively, of course. Raj Kapoor used the word 'taxi' to describe his brother when he was desperately trying to get dates from Shashi Kapoor for *Satyam Shivam Sundaram*[1]—a film that ostensibly explores the distinction between physical and spiritual love, but, in fact, represents Raj's love for the singer, Lata Mangeshkar. While actors were queuing up to play the lead role in the film, Raj strongly felt only Shashi could play his younger self in this somewhat autobiographical tale. So he looked at his brother's schedule and coolly appropriated all the dates he had given other filmmakers. 'He also insisted that on the days I was to shoot with him, I wouldn't shoot with anyone else,' Shashi tells film critic, Deepa Gahlot. 'To accommodate Rajji, I had to work round the clock, doing four to five shifts a day, sleeping in a car.'[2] His frenetic lifestyle, which made a car his semi-permanent address, led to the nickname, 'taxi'.

But 'taxi' came to become Shashi's moniker for other reasons,

too. Author Bunny Reuben suggests that both Shashi and Zeenat
Aman (Shashi's co-star in *Satyam Shivam Sundaram*) were subject
to Raj's tongue-lashing when he learnt of their shooting calendars.
'You people aren't stars,' Raj scolded. 'You are all taxis. Someone
puts your meter down—you go there! Then someone else puts
your meter down—and you go there. Two hours here…two hours
elsewhere. Taxis! That's what you artists have become.'[3]

Shashi Kapoor, one of the busiest stars of the 1970s. Courtesy: Merchant-Ivory Productions.

The pain of his older brother and father-figure publicly
admonishing him stayed with Shashi for many years. 'That hurt
him,' Madhu Jain says. 'He was very sensitive, he would never
forget anybody who said anything about him, especially if it was
Raj Kapoor.'

All the same, there was little Shashi could do to change his film schedule. The late 1970s—the decade that would define Shashi's career in India—would see the actor taking on a mind-boggling number of projects, hopping from studio to studio and playing a range of characters. In fact, Samir Ganguli, who directed the star in *Sharmeelee*,[4] says that the shift system in Hindi cinema started because of Shashi. '[He] was one of the busiest actors in those days,' he contends.[5]

Despite an overfull diary, Shashi never let his directors down. Samir states, '[He was] absolutely punctual. At times, because of his hectic schedules, he would get delayed, but none of us would really mind because we knew that once he arrived on the sets, he would never hesitate to deliver what was required of him.'[6]

But Shashi's chock-full roster came with a definite drawback—one that Neetu, who acted in ten films with the star, got to witness first-hand. 'I was very young and I joined the industry at a phase when we did really bad movies together,' she says. 'We would do three shifts. I didn't know main *kiska* character *kar rahi hoon, kya kar rahi hoon.* (I didn't know what character I was playing, what I was doing.) Shashi Uncle also would come to the sets and ask, "*Haan kya linein hai?*" ("So what are the lines?")'

A harried Shashi, who could barely keep pace with his film commitments, found it near-impossible to stay abreast of plots or characters. Sanjna Kapoor remembers learning of this during long family drives from South Bombay to Juhu to visit Prithviraj Kapoor. 'When Papaji was alive—and every Sunday we'd go to see him, if my dad was in town—I would ask my father to narrate the story of a film he was acting in. And he would make it up. He had no idea. He had absolutely no clue!'

If the 1970s saw Shashi at his busiest, the decade also saw him acting in films that were exceptionally violent and regressive. *Chor Machaye Shor*[7]—one of the few films Shashi acted in with Mumtaz—is packed with truly offensive situations. In fact, as critic Todd Stadtman points out, it has 'something of an obsession with rape'.[8] Vijay (Shashi) is thrown into jail on a trumped-up charge of raping his girlfriend, Rekha (Mumtaz). When he escapes prison, he decides that since he has been falsely implicated, he may as well prove his accusers right—leading to a horrifying scene where Vijay declares his intention to rape his girlfriend. Soon after, Rekha, attempting to shame Vijay, bares her breasts to him, and Vijay, 'proving himself to a good Indian boy, immediately covers his eyes and insists she cover up'[9]—making this, at once, a wholly unintelligible and terribly disquieting film. While there are a few bearable moments, entirely on account of the songs— 'Ghungroo Ki Tarah'[10] and 'Ek Daal Par Tota Bole',[11] among others—the shock ending, where our 'hero' wins his girlfriend's fidelity after attempting revenge-rape, erodes whatever little the music could salvage.

Then, there is the exceptionally bad *Immaan Dharam*[12]—one of the many Salim (Khan)–Javed (Akhtar) scripted films Shashi Kapoor acted in—that even the audiences rejected, making it the only flop for the scriptwriting duo. The plot is patchwork of inexplicable events—a blind Shyamlee (Aparna Sen) is almost raped; an alcoholic Jenny (Helen) is compelled to meet her fate and die; and touts Mohan (Shashi) and Ahmed (Amitabh Bachchan) become penitents on the path to contrition, thanks to a self-righteous Kabir (Sanjeev Kumar).

Sanjna, on catching her father in these films, says, 'I remember asking my mother, "How could he work in such crap?" Really, I am not a great feminist, but there is a whole period of Hindi cinema which upsets me so much—not only the violence, but also the way women are treated.' Then, Jennifer Kendal Kapoor explained to Sanjna that her father would have continued being a stage actor if it were financially viable. 'But he had a family and the family expanded. With that, the lifestyle changed and got cushier. If you decide to go to London every summer, and maintain a house in Goa, you have to earn a certain amount of money. You are sucked into this cycle and you can't get out.'

Anil Dharker goes on to say, 'I think Shashi took everything in his stride. He accepted it right from the beginning—this is what commercial cinema used to be and when you said "yes" to a role, you did what was asked.'

While the 1970s were littered with a number of forgettable films starring Shashi, there were a few watchable ones, too, among them *Sharmeelee*. This is undeniably Raakhee's film since she plays a double role, but the movie also managed to establish Shashi as a star, giving him a chance to show off his uber-charming self while singing 'Khilte Hain Gul Yahan',[13] 'Oh Meri Sharmeelee'[14] and the heartbreaking 'Kaise Kahen Hum'.[15] Besides, he also gets to display his acting range, as he transforms from a young man in love, to an alcoholic who is crushed when married to the wrong twin, to a spouse who learns to overcome his prejudice.

If I remember *Sharmeelee*, it is also for personal reasons—I skipped a school play rehearsal to catch the film with some friends at Regal Cinema in Connaught Place, Delhi. While I did not tell my mother, somehow she learnt—as parents often do—that I had played hookey. And she was disappointed—not because I had bunked a class, but because I had chosen to conceal the truth from her. To date, when I watch *Sharmeelee*, it is coloured by memories of that time.

*

If the 1970s were a significant decade in Shashi Kapoor's career, it was also because three associations grew in strength—with Shabana Azmi, Amitabh Bachchan, and Yash Chopra.

Shabana's first commercial film—after a National Award-winning debut in *Ankur*[16]—was with Shashi in *Fakira*,[17] an odd James Bond-inspired tacky thriller and comedy. Shabana says, 'Shashi and his wife had watched *Ankur* and had really liked my work,' suggesting that perhaps, the Kapoors had recommended her for her first commercial film foray. 'But never in my life did I dream that I would be working opposite this man. I had always seen him as a fan.'

Under Shashi's guidance, Shabana, for the first time, learnt the brass tacks of mainstream cinema. While shooting for *Fakira* in Kashmir, Shabana—a gold medallist in acting from Poona's Film and Television Institute of India (FTII)—struggled to look at light reflectors. 'If we were doing an outdoor scene—whether it was dramatic or romantic or sad—my eyes would be closed,' she tells me. 'And tears would stream down my face.' Shashi, who had known Shabana since her teenage years, and was twelve years older, often adopted a mock-angry tone with her in the presence of others—not unlike a brother ticking off a younger sister he respected, yet found fault with; now, he scolded: '*Itna bada gold medal le kar fayada kya hai? Ankhein nahin khol sakti ho?*' ('What is the use of winning such a major gold medal? Can't you open your eyes?') Then, he taught her how to watch the reflectors. 'He made me stare and stare, until I got used to it,' she says, while describing the process as pure 'torture'.

Then, Shashi taught her about top lighting, which, under the wrong circumstances, can make an actor's eyes disappear and give her a ghost-like appearance. 'He told me, if you have to shoot with a top light, you have to tilt your face upwards, so that there is less of a shadow,' Shabana says. 'There were many technical details I learnt from him.'

The 1970s phase of Shashi's career must also be acknowledged because it witnessed the birth of a phenomenon that came to be known as Shashitabh—Shashi and Amitabh would become one of the most successful two-hero combinations in Indian cinematic history.

How did the pairing come to be? 'I have no idea why producers and directors chose us as a team,' Amitabh confesses. 'I guess we looked like brothers and the success of some of the films we did added to the strength of the pairing.' Ramesh Talwar, who was the chief assistant director for *Deewaar*,[18] adds, 'Directors get used to working with the same actors. The moment a good role is written, the first thing many directors consider is how to work again with their favourite stars—that is how casting operates. They think, "This is *my* actor and *this* role will be perfect for his acting style." Even Satyajit Ray followed the pattern, as he often cast Soumitra Chatterjee in a range of roles.'

Shashi and Amitabh acted together in fourteen films—including, strangely enough, as twins in Manmohan Desai's *Suhaag*[19]—and Shashi soon came to be referred to as Amitabh's favourite heroine. Without a doubt, it is a sexist remark, but it is also meant to be a comment on Shashi's soft features and good looks, and the fact that he played warm-hearted, positive characters, as opposed to the brooding roles Amitabh embraced. Director Karan Johar points this out in the foreword to this book, when he refers to Shashi's persona of 'quiet graciousness and gentleness', and writes that he was often cast as 'an antidote to the "revenge or nothing" phase that Bollywood seemed to be passing through'. Amitabh goes on to say: 'Shashiji was an incredibly handsome man, and suited such roles better. That is why directors and writers gave him the parts that he did. I would imagine that the dark, troubled character suited me better!' Not surprisingly, Amitabh's persona earned him the sobriquet of an 'angry young man'.

The first of Shashi and Amitabh's appearances (if not a strong pairing) was in the multi-star production, *Roti Kapada Aur Makaan*[20]—a strangely structured film in which Mohan Babu (Shashi), the well-to-do boss of a struggling but ambitious Sheetal (Zeenat Aman), woos her before realizing that she is supposed to be a jobless Bharat's (Manoj Kumar) fiancée. Forming a foil to this story is a predictably angry Amitabh—playing Bharat's younger brother and a patriotic army man, Vijay—who learns that the brother he idolized has now become successful by turning into a don! While both Shashi and Amitabh have enjoyable roles, the tragedy is that they hardly share any screen time.

In this large ensemble cast, it is evident that Shashi is the real 'star'—a fact that Manoj Kumar goes out of his way to acknowledge in the opening credits of the film which read the main actors' names, followed by a separate slide that announces: 'And Above All Shashi Kapoor'.

That Shashi is the 'star' is further emphasized by his exceptionally fine clothes—sharp suits and ties that, according to Anil Dharker, were designed by Jennifer Kendal Kapoor. When Shashi's Mohan Babu asks Sheetal to marry him, he dons a white suit and a red silk tie with black polka dots; and during his engagement ceremony, he changes his tie to one that has large orange dots against a white background. 'Jennifer had this thing that we call taste,' Anil says. 'Very refined taste. That influence rubbed off on Shashi.'

Finally, there's Shashi's thriving association with his friend and master director, Yash Chopra; under his expert direction, the chemistry between Amitabh and Shashi came to be exploited in a series of blockbuster films, starting with *Deewaar*.

Deewaar (1975)

After the success of *Waqt*,[21] Yash Chopra wanted to cast Shashi Kapoor in *Aadmi Aur Insaan*[22] and *Ittefaq*.[23] Unfortunately, Shashi had already started overcommitting himself and was not available for either film. Finally, a decade after *Waqt*, Yash and Shashi got to work together in what is considered one of the most iconic films of Hindi cinema, *Deewaar*. Shashi was to act as an upright cop enlisted to chase a reckless criminal, played by Amitabh Bachchan; unbeknownst to him, the criminal was his brother.

However, it took a while for the stars to align and for all the casting-chips to fall in place. For one, *Deewaar*'s producer, Gulshan Rai, was keen to cast Rajesh Khanna—who had played the lead in Yash's hit film, *Daag*,[24] and who was clearly the biggest star of the late 1960s and early 1970s—in the role of the mobster. But Yash had seen Amitabh in *Zanjeer*[25] and wanted him to play the part; with some difficulty, Yash managed to get Gulshan to relent.

Then, there was Shashi. While Yash had been waiting to cast him in a film for some time, Gulshan again needed some convincing, not just from the director, but also from the scriptwriters, Salim–Javed—who, having delivered hit after hit, wielded sufficient power to influence a film's casting process. 'We fought over Shashi saab because, though he was a senior actor, [he was] older [than] Amitabh and we wanted him to play the younger brother in *Deewaar*,' Javed Akhtar tells journalist, Rajiv Vijayakar. 'We knew he could do it, and even Shashi was not [as] confident [as we were]! And we had to convince producer Gulshan Rai.'[26] At last, their efforts bore fruit.

While Shashi had been named Vijay in *Waqt*, he was called Ravi in *Deewaar*, and Amitabh was referred to as Vijay (as in *Roti Kapada Aur Makaan*). The names became so popular that they stuck even when the two did not work in Yash's films.

The casting decision—of having Shashi assume the more 'noble' role, and Amitabh, the more passionate one—has made critics and audiences comment that Amitabh is the more memorable of the two in *Deewaar*. However, Ramesh Sippy, who would later direct the two actors in *Shaan*,[27] points out that such comparisons fail to appreciate the conscious decisions Shashi had to make as an actor: 'If Shashi had to play that role [in *Deewaar*] and be sincere to it, he had to underplay it. [...] However, if he had tried to stand out as a performer and give the kind of performance that gives you stardom, he would not have done justice to the role. [...] He did it right.'[28]

Interestingly, even while being privy to these opposing assessments of his performance, Shashi remained unflappable.

Sharmila Tagore says, 'He always had a sense of humour. He had no problem being Amitabh Bachchan's "number two" in *Deewaar* or elsewhere.'

Above all, *Deewaar*'s casting decisions paved the way for a solid friendship between Shashi and Amitabh. 'We had a lot of fun together,' Shashi says. Once, while judging a beauty contest in Poona, where Zeenat Aman was also an arbiter, Shashi and Amitabh got so drunk that they could not decide which woman to pick as the winner. Shashi adds, 'They all looked lovely to us. We thought they all should win prizes.'[29] Eventually, Zeenat, who had been a beauty queen, stepped in and made a decision for the tipsy actors. This would be one of several spontaneous moments of good cheer between the two stars.

Today, *Deewaar* is considered a departure from most of Yash's other films, since it lacks a strong romantic structure. Amitabh/Vijay's girlfriend is Parveen Babi/Anita and Shashi's character's love interest in the film is Veera, played by Neetu Singh. But the romantic moments are brief, often circling around songs, and do not interrupt the main plot. Neetu—who was dating Rishi Kapoor at that time—says, 'In *Deewaar*, Shashi Uncle and I had two songs and since they were romantic, they didn't need choreographers. There was "Keh Doon Tumhe"[30]—which was very popular, and even now plays in all the hotspots—and "Maine Tujhe Maanga, Tujhe Paya Hai".[31] Usually, back then, one song would take two or three days to picturize. But—and I am not joking—we finished filming both songs in one-and-a-half days! That's the way Yashji worked. He was known to be very, very quick.'

If *Deewaar* is remembered, it is not only for the cast, but also for the writing expertise of Salim–Javed (who were working with Yash for the first time) and Shashi's/Ravi's classic four-word retort to Amitabh's/Vijay's long monologue towards the end of the film—the unforgettable, '*Mere paas maa hai!*' ('I have our mother'). A lot of thought went into writing this high-impact punchline. 'Ravi could have said all kinds of things..."*Aaj mere paas maa ka pyar hai, mujhe yeh mil gaya, mujhe voh mil gaya*" ("Today I have my mother's love, I've got this and I've got that"),' Javed tells director and author, Nasreen Munni Kabir. 'By contrast, take Vijay [...] who is providing the platform for this punchline. He has many lines before Ravi makes his mark with a single statement. Perhaps Ravi's dialogue wouldn't have worked without Vijay's monologue.' He adds, 'You have to orchestrate a scene. If you try to bombard the listener's sensibilities all the time, his sensibility will be [so] shattered that when you want him to feel something, he will be [...] tired.'[32]

The famous scene between Amitabh/Vijay and Shashi/Ravi was shot at Rajkamal Studios. 'Little did I know—and neither did any other person connected with the film—that the scene and its dialogues would become popular,' Amitabh says. While the long soliloquy was thoroughly rehearsed for the appropriate impact, Amitabh says that this was hardly an indication that the scene would become part of Indian film history: 'As professionals, yes, we do rehearse. But that is normal amongst artists.'

Later, at the premiere of *Deewaar*, Amitabh sat next to Shashi. Amitabh recalls:

> We never said a word. But [at] the '*mere pass maa hai*' moment, I felt a gentle hand on mine. It was Shashiji's. He never spoke, but the way he held my hand said everything. It was reassurance, it was affection, it was acknowledgement, it was complimentary, it was appreciation, it was everything that a struggling actor that had once played an extra in a film that starred this gentleman sitting next to him [in James Ivory's *Bombay Talkie*] had never ever dreamt would happen.[33]

Deewaar would earn box office and critical acclaim, and win Filmfare Awards for Shashi (best supporting actor), Yash (best director) and Salim–Javed (best screenplay, story and dialogue), besides being recognized as the best film of the year. It would become a golden jubilee hit and then run for another fifty weeks— becoming one of the biggest blockbusters of Hindi cinema.

Kabhi Kabhie (1976)

In 1976, Yash Chopra released *Kabhi Kabhie*,[34] his ultimate ode to romance, with a huge multi-star cast that included Shashi Kapoor, Amitabh Bachchan, Raakhee, Waheeda Rahman, Rishi Kapoor, Neetu Singh, Simi Garewal and Parikshit Sahni.

Kabhi Kabhie tells the story of a poet, Amit, and his love-interest, Pooja, who keep alive memories of their passionate affair, even while being compelled to marry against their wishes; years later, their pasts collide through their children.

While the multi-generational plot feels long-drawn-out, convoluted and melodramatic, there are touches in the film that are beautiful—the songs, for instance, are memorable, especially the title track, which Amitabh (as Amit) sings to his love interest Raakhee (as Pooja), who in turns sings it to Shashi (as Vijay) when she marries him. Then, there are romantic scenes in Kashmir, with Amitabh's soulful voice reciting poetry. (Kashmir's landscapes, from this point in time, would become a Yash staple, until the director discovered the icy crests of the Swiss Alps.) Finally, one can't help being struck by the organic feel of the film—with characters living in real homes (as against inhabiting mock studio sets), and often wearing their own clothes. 'Yashji did not want us to hire a costume designer,' Neetu tells me. 'He would say, "You wear what you would in real life. I don't want it to be filmy."'

While *Kabhi Kabhie* was inspired by Yash's friend and regular lyricist, Sahir Ludhianvi (Amitabh's Amit was modelled on him), Shashi's Vijay was loosely based on Yash himself—the jovial man who secretly aspire to be a poet and displayed a kind of open-mindedness. In fact, Yash's wife, Pamela Chopra, says, 'As far as

Shashi's characters in most of his films go, starting with *Deewaar*, they were loosely based on Yash. My husband felt closest to Shashi since their temperaments matched. He personally developed Shashi's character in *Kabhi Kabhie* because Vijay was the way Yash was.'

Then there is Vijay's relationship with his son, Vikram, which bore strong parallels with Yash's association with his own sons, Aditya and Uday. Rishi, who would play Vikram, says, 'Even today people talk about Vikram and Vijay, but back in the mid-1970s, a father and his son having a slap-on-the-back relationship was unheard of.'

It was a smart casting plan—to offer the role of Vikram to a young member of the Kapoor family. But Rishi dithered over accepting it because by the time *Kabhi Kabhie* was to be made, he had gained in star status and had a considerable fan following, with two hits alongside his then girlfriend, Neetu—*Khel Khel Mein*[35] and *Rafoo Chakkar*.[36] He was rather reluctant to act in a multi-star film. Shashi jokingly says, 'Yash called me up to say Rishi is not doing the film. I said, let's beat him up.'[37]

When he was finally coerced into accepting the role, Rishi found working with his 'chacha' a huge learning experience. He says, 'I remember, once, Shashi Uncle commented on my acting: "*Tum react nahin karte ho.* (You don't react.) You are very good with your lines but you must react also." Back then, I didn't know what he was trying to say. I felt that I didn't have to react without cause or deliver loud expressions. *Jaise aadmi life main react karta hai naa, waisa hona chahiye.* (Acting should mirror life.) But then, over the years, I understood what he meant. I saw that it was crucial for me to offer the right cues, so that the other actor could pick up on them and deliver his lines well. It helped me, as an actor, to learn this from Shashi Uncle.'

Kabhi Kabhie was a box office success, running in theatres for fifty weeks and earning the golden jubilee stamp. To date, it remains an iconic film, appreciated for its contemporary spirit, and the fact that both Shashi and Amitabh, for the first time, play older men with complex pasts.

Doosra Aadmi (1977)

For his debut film as director, Ramesh Talwar worked under his mentor's banner, Yash Raj Films. This would be the first movie that Yash Chopra would produce with another director.

As with *Kabhi Kabhie*, *Doosra Aadmi*[38] is packed with a star cast that includes Rishi Kapoor, Neetu Singh, Raakhee and Shashi Kapoor. It tells the story of an older woman (Raakhee playing Nisha) enamoured by a younger married man who reminds her of her dead boyfriend.

Ramesh was adamant that he didn't want to give Rishi a double role as the dead boyfriend and the married man—such a casting decision, he felt, would make the plot altogether obvious. Instead, he wanted a star who looked similar to Rishi to play the deceased lover. While he was mulling over possibilities, he happened to spot a photo of Rishi in *The Illustrated Weekly of India*, soon after *Kabhi Kabhie* had been shot, with a caption that read that Rishi looked strikingly like his uncle, Shashi. 'That inspired me,' Ramesh says. 'I took that picture of Rishi with me and went to see Shashi.'

When Ramesh told Shashi that he wished to offer him a guest role as Nisha's late boyfriend, the actor was hesitant. Ramesh says, 'He told me, "Look, I have never accepted a guest role so far. I didn't even do it for Manmohan Desai." But Shashi was willing to hear a narration of the script. "If the role adds value to the plot, I will do it," he said. "But if I don't think it is the right fit for me, and if I say no, don't get upset or angry."'

So, one morning, Ramesh had breakfast with Shashi at the latter's home and then shared a car from South Bombay to Natraj Studio in Andheri. Along the way, the story of *Doosra Aadmi* was narrated. By the end of the drive, Shashi had agreed to do the film. 'His one condition was that we could not use his name in the film's publicity material,' Ramesh says. 'He wanted the audience to be surprised, just as he had been when I had narrated the shock twist.'

When the film hit theatres, the audiences were certainly taken in! They liked the melodious songs (including 'Aao Manayen Jashn-E-Mohabbat'[39] and 'Ankhon Mein Kajal Hai',[40] all composed by Rajesh Roshan), beautiful stars and a plot suffused with Yash's proclivities—which made *Doosra Aadmi* a clear Yash Raj production. And they *especially* loved Shashi. 'People would jump off their seats when Shashi would first appear in the frame singing "Yeh Kya Mastiyan" from the hit song "Kya Mausam Hai"[41],' Ramesh says.

If there were objections to the film, they came from small towns, especially in Punjab and Haryana, on account of Raakhee's character—a woman who smoked and drank in bars. 'At that time, Raakhee was in a film called *Tapasya*,[42] where she was quite pious,' Ramesh says. 'A few people couldn't accept a star like her, with a recent history of rather devout roles, smoking and drinking. While I personally didn't find Raakhee's character odd—possibly a function of my modern sensibilities, and the fact that all my female friends used to drink—small-town India thought differently.'

Despite Punjab and Haryana's lukewarm feedback, *Doosra Aadmi* did good business at the box office, running in some theatres for a hundred days.

Trishul (1978)

Starting with *Waqt*, and then *Kabhi Kabhie*, Yash Chopra made it a point to situate his characters in Delhi (not Bombay), perhaps because he wanted them to appear earthy and real, as opposed to out-of-the-world and 'filmy'. *Trishul*,[43] consequently, unspooled in the neighbourhoods of New Delhi.

After *Deewaar*, *Trishul* was the second Salim–Javed scripted film directed by Yash. Once more, Amitabh Bachchan and Shashi Kapoor were given key roles, this time as half-brothers (with different mothers and the same father). Once more, Amitabh's character (named—what else?—Vijay) is sombre and surly, motivated, as he is, by a sense of revenge—for, his father abandoned his pregnant mother. And once more, Shashi (cast as—no, not Ravi—but Shekhar) is likeable, unable to fathom Vijay's streak of vindictiveness as he rises from penury to challenge his father's businesses.

Unlike *Deewaar*'s somewhat lean structure, *Trishul* feels bloated with the over-the-top histrionics of actors like Sanjeev Kumar (playing the two-timing father), and far too many actors—including Raakhee cast as Vijay's love interest; Hema Malini as the businesswoman Shekhar falls for; and a younger generation played by Poonam Dhillon and Sachin. However, regardless of these shortcomings, *Trishul* was a huge hit, running in theatres for seventy-five weeks and then playing as a matinee show for much longer.

Today, *Trishul* is not only referred to by popular filmmakers—including Anurag Kashyap in his classic *Gangs of Wasseypur*[44]—but is also remembered as the movie that strengthened Shashi's association with Amitabh after *Deewaar*. During filming, both were put up at the Oberoi Intercontinental Hotel in South Delhi, and they had ample opportunity to fraternize at night. 'We did spend a lot of time together after work at the only disco in town, Tabela, within the hotel,' Amitabh says. 'And yes, sometimes, when it would get late, we would go to shoot immediately from there.'

This is corroborated by Yash who was rarely part of the merriment at Tabela since he was a teetotaller: 'One night, Amitabh and Shashi went out partying and [when] they came back to the hotel at 6.30 in the morning, I had the unit ready to leave for shooting.' He adds, 'I didn't realize that they had just come in. They had no choice but to go straight to the film, snoozing in the breaks.'[45]

The duo's fondness for this now-deceased Delhi hotspot can be more fully appreciated in Amitabh's interview with Madhu Jain; here, the actor says: 'As a student it was always a dream to go [to Tabela] and I never had the opportunity.' As for Shashi, he got to do what he loved doing—'Shashi was a good dancer,' Amitabh says.[46] It was during this time of drinking, dancing and jubilation that Shashi and Amitabh become close friends.

Kaala Patthar (1979)

Another multi-star action drama, with six lead actors—Amitabh Bachchan, Raakhee, Shashi Kapoor, Praveen Babi, Shatrughan Sinha and Neetu Singh—*Kaala Patthar*[47] had (expectedly) been scripted by Salim–Javed. Once again, Amitabh, as Vijay, plays the angry young man, this time with a dark secret. Once again, Shashi, as Ravi, plays an eager, rather likeable bloke, this time as an engineer in charge of a coal mine.

Notwithstanding the obvious similarities with past ventures, *Kaala Patthar* is a clear departure from Yash Chopra's films. For one, Shashi has a chance to grow into more than an affable character, with several scenes demanding that he express his frustration with the hostile working conditions in the mines; his dialogues with the coal mine owner, Dhanraaj, played by Prem Chopra, throb with anger.

For another, *Kaala Patthar* could be referred to as India's first disaster film, based on the December 1975 catastrophe in the Chasanala charcoal mine in Dhanbad, which got flooded with water and trapped more than 500 workers. It is also the Hindi film industry's response (naturally with songs and romance) to such successful Hollywood fare as *The Poseidon Adventure*[48] and *The Towering Inferno*.[49]

Finally, *Kaala Patthar* is in a class of its own for its sets, with art director, Sudhendu Roy, capturing the grittiness of the coal mines and their unfathomable blackness. To recreate the stark scenes inside the mines, sets were built in Film City, which was a relatively new studio back then, and an American technical team was called to monitor the effects.

Speaking of sets, while shooting *Kaala Patthar*, Yash commissioned Raj Kapoor's farm in Loni near Poona for some scenes. At that time, the town had only one major hotel, Blue Diamond (now a Taj Vivanta), with precisely one suite. Both Amitabh and Shashi expressed the desire to stay in that room. To manage a situation that could get out of hand, and to avoid accusations of partiality, Yash finally chose to stay in the large suite himself.

Kaala Patthar, for all its freshness and ingenuity, did not fare well at the box office. Its elaborate storyline, which thrashed reckless capitalism and celebrated the rise of the proletariat—a 'band of brothers' as it were—failed to entice an audience seeking escape. Moreover, the climactic scene was considered over-long and dilatory. Ramesh Talwar states that in the smaller towns, theatre owners themselves started editing the film for it to succeed. 'Then, major theatre owners began asking us for the permission, by first explaining why certain scenes looked too long,' he says. 'They would request us to send the editor.' Once trimmed, the film did manage to bounce back, to some degree, at the box office. But the recovery proved to be short-lived.

Silsila (1981)

Silsila[50] is essentially a romantic triangle involving Amitabh Bachchan (as Amit), Jaya Bachchan (née Bhaduri, as Shobha), and Rekha (as Chandni). Amit is in love with Chandni, but circumstances are such that he is compelled to abandon her, and watch her marry Dr Anand (Sanjeev Kumar)—the fourth piece of the romantic puzzle. Amit's decision is brought on by the sudden demise of his brother, Shekhar—a man who leaves behind him a bereaved fiancée, Shobha, who Amit is forced to marry.

Yash Chopra could think of nobody better suited to play Shekhar than his favourite actor and alter-ego, Shashi Kapoor. This would be Shashi's last of eight films with Yash. *Silsila* would also be the only film where Shashi would play Amitabh's older brother. And perhaps, because the film is not scripted by Salim–Javed but by Yash himself, Amitabh and Shashi are freed from the burden of playing characters named Vijay and Ravi. (Of course, this is after playing siblings Vijay and Ravi for the nth time in Ramesh Sippy's James Bond-inspired *Shaan*, scripted by Salim–Javed, and released just a little before *Silsila*.)

Silsila soars when Shashi and Amitabh share the screen, and there are some exuberant scenes between them—such as when they get drunk, or when they shower together, as men so often do in gyms in the West. In fact, this is the first Hindi film to show two of the industry's leading actors showering in the same frame as part of, what is, a very natural setting.

But after a plane crash, Shashi's character abruptly departs from the story, and *Silsila* loses some of its high energy and joie de vivre. What follows now is a complex, emotionally wrenching plot, with very adult characters, an extramarital affair involving Amit and Chandni, and devastating consequences—a solemnity that is broken only occasionally with songs such as the Holi hit, 'Rang Barse'.[51]

Prior to the release of the film, there was a lot of speculation in the media about whether the choice of actors had anything to do with the lead stars' real-life connections. But tabloid gossip did not translate into financial returns for the film—*Silsila* did not fare well at the box office. Pamela Chopra concedes that the film may have been 'a tad bit different'; in other words, it was ahead of its times. She says: 'Marriage is a very, very sacred institution in India, and when the director created sympathy for the two lovers who were willing to go outside their marriage and continue their love affair, he didn't carry the audience with him.'[52]

Nonetheless, today, *Silsila* is viewed as a cult film. And Shashi, despite his bit-role, is remembered for such lines as: '*Hum gayab hone waalo mein se nahi hai. Jahan jahan se guzharte hai jalwe dikhate hai. Dost toh kya, dushman bhi yaad rakhte hai.*' ('I am not among those who vanish. Wherever I may wander, my lust for life follows me. I am here to be remembered, not only by friends, but also by adversaries.')

Notes

1. 1978, *Satyam Shivam Sundaram*, dir. Raj Kapoor, prod. Raj Kapoor, starring Shashi Kapoor, Zeenat Aman, Padmini Kolhapure.
2. Deepa Gahlot, Shashi Kapoor, *The Prithviwallas* (New Delhi: Roli, 2004), p. 64.
3. Quoted in Bunny Reuben, *Dilip Kumar: Star Legend of Indian Cinema* (New Delhi: HarperCollins, 2004), p. 119.
4. 1971, *Sharmeelee*, dir. Samir Ganguly, prod. Subodh Mukherji, starring Shashi Kapoor, Raakhee, Nazir Hussain.
5. Quoted in Surekha Kapada-Bose, 'Shashi Kapoor: Restricted but Unrelenting', *Dawn*, 9 April 2015.
6. *Ibid.*
7. 1974, *Chor Machaye Shor*, dir. Ashok Roy, prod. N.N. Sippy, starring Shashi Kapoor, Mumtaz, Danny Denzongpa.
8. Todd Stadtman, *Funky Bollywood: The Wild World of 1970s Indian Action Cinema* (Surrey: FAB Press, 2015), p. 102.
9. *Ibid.*
10. 'Ghungroo Ki Tarah', lyr. Ravindra Jain, comp. Ravindra Jain, artist Kishore Kumar.
11. 'Ek Daal Par Tota Bole', lyr. Indrajeet Singh Tulsi, comp. Ravindra Jain, artists Mohammed Rafi, Lata Mangeshkar.
12. 1977, *Immaan Dharam*, dir. Desh Mukherjee, prod. Premji, starring Amitabh Bachchan, Shashi Kapoor, Sanjeev Kumar, Rekha.
13. 'Khilte Hain Gul Yahan,' lyr. Neeraj, comp. S.D. Burman, artist Kishore Kumar.

14. 'Oh Meri Sharmeelee', lyr. Neeraj, comp. S.D. Burman, artist Kishore Kumar.

15. 'Kaise Kahen Hum', lyr. Neeraj, comp. S.D. Burman, artist Kishore Kumar.

16. 1974, *Ankur*, dir. Shyam Benegal, prod. Mohan J. Bijlani, Freni Variava, starring Shabana Azmi, Anant Nag, Sadhu Meher.

17. 1976, *Fakira*, dir. C.P. Dixit, prod. N.N. Sippy, starring Shashi Kapoor, Shabana Azmi, Danny Denzongpa.

18. 1975, *Deewaar*, dir. Yash Chopra, prod. Gulshan Rai, starring Amitabh Bachchan, Shashi Kapoor, Neetu Singh, Parveen Babi.

19. 1979, *Suhaag*, dir. Manmohan Desai, prod. Rajinder Kumar Sharma, Shakti Subhash Sharma, Prakash Trehan, starring Amitabh Bachchan, Shashi Kapoor, Rekha, Parveen Babi.

20. 1974, *Roti Kapada Aur Makaan*, dir. Manoj Kumar, prod. Manoj Kumar, starring Manoj Kumar, Shashi Kapoor, Amitabh Bachchan, Zeenat Aman.

21. 1965, *Waqt*, dir. Yash Chopra, prod. B.R. Chopra, starring Balraj Sahni, Sharmila Tagore, Shashi Kapoor.

22. 1969, *Aadmi Aur Insaan*, dir. Yash Chopra, prod. B.R. Chopra, starring Dharmendra, Saira Banu, Feroz Khan.

23. 1969, *Ittefaq*, dir. Yash Chopra, prod. B.R. Chopra, starring Rajesh Khanna, Nanda, Madan Puri.

24. 1973, *Daag*, dir. Yash Chopra, prod. Yash Chopra, starring Sharmila Tagore, Rajesh Khanna, Raakhee.

25. 1973, *Zanjeer*, dir. Prakash Mehra, prod. Prakash Mehra, starring Amitabh Bachchan, Jaya Bhaduri, Pran.

26. Rajiv Vijayakar, 'Never Before, Never Again: The Shashi Kapoor-Amitabh Bachchan Chemistry', *Bollywood Hungama*, in <http://www.bollywoodhungama.com/movies/features/type/view/id/8260/>, accessed on 24 December 2015.

27. 1980, *Shaan*, dir. Ramesh Sippy, prod. G.P. Sippy, starring Sunil Dutt, Amitabh Bachchan, Shashi Kapoor, Raakhee, Parveen Babi.

28. Quoted in Madhu Jain, *The Kapoors: The First Family of Indian Cinema* (New Delhi: Penguin, 2005), p. 236.

29. Quoted in Jessica Hines, *Looking for the Big B: Bollywood, Bachchan and Me* (London: Bloomsbury, 2007), p. 102.

30. 'Keh Doon Tumhe', lyr. Sahir Ludhianvi, comp. R.D. Burman, artists Asha Bhosle, Kishore Kumar.

31. 'Maine Tujhe Maanga, Tujhe Paya Hai', lyr. Sahir Ludhianvi, comp. R.D. Burman, artists Asha Bhosle, Kishore Kumar.

32. Nasreen Munni Kabir, *Talking Films: Conversations on Hindi Cinema with Javed Akhtar* (New Delhi: Oxford University Press, 2006), p. 43.
33. Quoted in 'I Asked Shashi for a Job: Amitabh', *The Times of India*, 17 September 2009.
34. 1976, *Kabhi Kabhie*, dir. Yash Chopra, prod. Yash Chopra, starring Amitabh Bachchan, Shashi Kapoor, Raakhee, Simi Garewal, Waheeda Rehman, Rishi Kapoor, Neetu Singh.
35. 1975, *Khel Khel Mein*, dir. Ravi Tandon, prod. Ravi Malhotra, starring Rishi Kapoor, Neetu Singh, Rakesh Roshan.
36. 1975, *Rafoo Chakkar*, dir. Narender Bedi, prod. I.A. Nadiadwala, starring Rishi Kapoor, Neetu Singh, Madan Puri.
37. Quoted in Rachel Dwyer, *Yash Chopra: Fifty Years of Indian Cinema* (New Delhi: Roli, 2002).
38. 1977, *Doosra Aadmi*, dir. Ramesh Talwar, prod. Yash Chopra, starring Rishi Kapoor, Raakhee, Shashi Kapoor, Neetu Singh.
39. 'Aao Manayen Jashn-E-Mohabbat', lyr. Majrooh Sultanpuri, comp. Rajesh Roshan, artists Kishore Kumar, Lata Mangeshkar.
40. 'Ankhon Mein Kajal Hai', lyr. Majrooh Sultanpuri, comp. Rajesh Roshan, artists Kishore Kumar, Lata Mangeshkar.
41. 'Kya Mausam Hai', lyr. Majrooh Sultanpuri, comp. Rajesh Roshan, artists Kishore Kumar, Lata Mangeshkar, Mohammed Rafi.
42. 1976, *Tapasya*, dir. Anil Ganguly, prod. Tarachand Barjatya, starring Parikshit Sahni, Raakhee, Asrani.
43. 1978, *Trishul*, dir. Yash Chopra, prod. Gulshan Rai, starring Amitabh Bachchan, Shashi Kapoor, Hema Malini, Raakhee.
44. 2012, *Gangs of Wasseypur*, dir. Anurag Kashyap, prod. Anurag Kashyap, Sunil Bohra, Vikram Malhotra, Guneet Monga, starring Manoj Bajpai, Nawazuddin Siddiqui, Huma Qureshi.
45. Quoted in Rachel Dwyer, *Yash Chopra: Fifty Years of Indian Cinema* (New Delhi: Roli, 2002), p. 106.
46. Quoted in Madhu Jain, *The Kapoors: The First Family of Indian Cinema* (New Delhi: Penguin, 2005), p. 249.
47. 1979, *Kaala Patthar*, dir. Yash Chopra, prod. Yash Chopra, starring Amitabh Bachchan, Shashi Kapoor, Shatrughan Sinha, Neetu Singh, Parveen Babi.
48. 1972, *The Poseidon Adventure*, dir. Ronald Neame, prod. Irwin Allen, starring Gene Hackman, Ernest Borgnine, Red Buttons.
49. 1974, *The Towering Inferno*, dir. John Guillermin, prod. Irwin Allen, starring Steve McQueen, Paul Newman, William Holden.

50. 1981, *Silsila*, dir. Yash Chopra, prod. Yash Chopra, starring Amitabh Bachchan, Shashi Kapoor, Sanjeev Kumar, Rekha, Jaya Bhaduri.

51. 'Rang Barse', lyr. Harivanshrai Bachchan, comp. Shiv–Hari, singer Amitabh Bachchan.

52. Quoted in Tejaswini Ganti, *Producing Bollywood: Inside the Contemporary Hindi Film Industry* (North Carolina: Duke University Press, 2012), p. 284.

5

ON THE MONEY
Shashi, the Producer and Businessman

'You have to remember, Dad did not ever say, "I want to be a film star,"' Kunal Kapoor tells me while we're talking about Shashi Kapoor. 'There are actors, people in the business, who are doing very well, and whose agenda it is to become stars. That wasn't Dad's plan.'

If we look past Shashi the 'star', we see a man who is enthused not just by the craft of acting, but by the nuts and bolts of post-production work. In this respect, he is like his eldest brother, Raj Kapoor, who saw himself not just as a 'hero' but as a filmmaker.

In the 1970s, Shashi launched a company, Vidushak Arts, which would rent out equipment and cameras. Shashi's venture provided a lifeline to several filmmakers—for, as things stood, they had to import most tools from overseas, but could do so only if they could show they were earning foreign exchange. 'One forgets how extraordinarily difficult it was to make films back then,' filmmaker Dev Benegal says. 'It's almost as though the state did not want you to make movies. There was a licence on importing negative film, sound editing equipment, cameras and lights. It was an impoverished state of affairs.'

Shashi was one of the early few to get a licence to import a flatbed editing machine—a Steenbeck—which Dev was fortunate to use. The Steenbeck was housed in the Bombay Film Laboratories—now an apartment building in Prabhadevi, Bombay—and a lot of talent would pass through, including Shyam Benegal (who used Vidushak Arts' equipment for some of his films) and Satyajit Ray's cinematographer, Subrata Mitra (who, as we know, shot a few of the early Merchant–Ivory movies).

Shashi—never a man to pursue just one dream—also hoped to bring the films he made directly to the audience, without having to depend on a nexus of distributors—who, in his view, were business-people first, with little appreciation for cinema as an art form. 'What do diamond merchants know about films?' Shashi asks. '[If I take over], instead of making a film and waiting for a distributor, I could do both at the same time.'[1]

The idea took root, and in the late 1960s, when he had to bail Ismail Merchant out of a cash crunch, he did it in exchange for the right to distribute *Bombay Talkie*[2] in India. Unfortunately, the Merchant–Ivory film did not do any remarkable business at the box office, and Shashi failed to make money.

Soon after, in the early 1970s, Shashi acquired the Indian distribution rights for an odd adults-only Japanese anime film, *A Thousand and One Nights* (*Sen'ya Ichiya Monogatari*),[3] directed by Eiichi Yamamoto and released as an X-rated movie in the US. Harking back to an age-old story, the film chronicles its hero, Aladdin's journey from rags to riches to rags, even as he dallies with a number of women—Miriam, a beautiful slave; the lusty Amazons; and Yahiz, who, it turns out, is his daughter. The psychedelic, erotically-charged movie, while a success in Japan, did poor business in India.

After two failures, Shashi's next big step as a film distributor was when he bought rights, within the territories of Delhi and Uttar Pradesh (UP), for Raj Kapoor's *Bobby*[4] (and later, *Satyam*

1970, *Bombay Talkie*. Shashi Kapoor's Vikram shot with his on-screen wife, Mala, played by Aparna Sen. Shashi will go on to produce Aparna's first directorial venture, *36 Chowringhee Lane* (1981).

Courtesy: Merchant–Ivory Productions.

1972, *Siddhartha*. Pinchoo Kapoor (as Kamaswami, the merchant) and Shashi Kapoor (in the title role) in Conrad Rooks' film based on Hermann Hesse's iconic novel.

Courtesy: Alexander Rooks/Lotus Films.

1978, *Junoon*. Shashi Kapoor's first production, directed by Shyam Benegal: an 1857 saga about a married Muslim man, Javed Khan (Shashi Kapoor) who falls in love with a young Anglo-Indian woman.

Courtesy: Shyam Benegal.

1983, *Heat and Dust*. Shashi Kapoor, the nawab. Here, he's seated during his royal durbar.
Courtesy: Merchant–Ivory Productions.

1983, *Heat and Dust*. A close-up of Shashi Kapoor as the nawab in James Ivory's film based on Ruth Prawer Jhabvala's Booker Prize-winning novel. *Courtesy*: Merchant–Ivory Productions.

1986, *New Delhi Times*. Shashi Kapoor in Ramesh Sharma's political thriller as the upright newspaper editor—a role that wins him his only National Award. Here, he's seated beside his on-screen lawyer-wife, played by Sharmila Tagore. *Courtesy*: Ramesh Sharma.

1987, *Sammy and Rosie Get Laid*. A Hanif Kureishi-scripted film that has Shashi Kapoor playing Rafi, a retired politician from Pakistan, who comes to London to visit his son, Sammy (Ayub Khan-Din, right).

1993, *In Custody*. Shashi Kapoor, as the broken, ageing poet Nur, in a private moment with his pigeons.
Courtesy: Merchant–Ivory Productions.

1993, *In Custody*. Ismail Merchant's first feature film as director. James Ivory, at his friend's behest, directs this scene where Om Puri's Deven interviews the poet Nur (Shashi Kapoor) for a literary magazine.

Courtesy: Merchant–Ivory Productions.

1998, *Jinnah*. Pakistan's answer to Richard Attenborough's *Gandhi*, where Shashi Kapoor as an angel (or a 'narrator') walks Muhammad Ali Jinnah (Christopher Lee) through his life.

Courtesy: Jamil Dehlavi.

1998, *Side Streets*. As a has-been Bollywood actor, Shashi Kapoor's Vikram Raj, stranded in New York City.

Photo credit: Seth Rubin. *Courtesy*: Side Streets Productions.

Shivam Sundaram).[5] For Raj, his brother's intervention was a welcome relief. After the box office failure of *Mera Naam Joker*,[6] he had a tough time convincing distributors to buy the rights for *Bobby*—a film that seemed to have nothing going for it, with two newcomers as protagonists—twenty-one-year-old Rishi Kapoor (in his first lead role after a cameo in *Mera Naam Joker*) and sixteen-year-old Dimple Kapadia.

For Shashi, the move to distribute this film was part-strategic, part-instinctive. 'He wanted to make money,' Rishi says. 'Shashi Uncle was confident that *Bobby* would be a big hit. He restored confidence in his brother by saying, "I know this picture will be a blockbuster!"'

Shashi's conviction may have sprung from the fact that *Bobby* relates a story that never seems to tire—a rich boy (Rishi as Raj) falls in love with a poor girl (Dimple as Bobby) and surmounts all odds, from parental opposition to abduction attempts, to emerge triumphant. Besides, it's hard to remain impervious to the on-screen chemistry between the lead actors, and the catchy songs by Laxmikant–Pyarelal—for the first time, Raj happened to work with composers other than Shankar–Jaikishan.

Shashi's predictions proved to be spot on. *Bobby* was a huge hit. Overnight, the film made stars of Rishi and Dimple. When Rishi's plane landed in Delhi, Shashi arranged for nearly 500 young girls on the tarmac to welcome his nephew, who screamed the young actor's name while holding posters of *Bobby*. 'It was such a big thing for me,' Rishi tells me. 'Of course, I was Shashi Uncle's nephew and I was hogging all the limelight—what with Dimple being preoccupied post-marriage (she had wedded superstar, Rajesh Khanna, soon after the film's shoot). The newspapers were full of stories that Rishi Kapoor was in town. And the Escorts bike in the film—I rode a similar bike from the airport, and it created quite a stir.'

Unfortunately, *Bobby*'s box office success and the young stars'

popularity did not translate into big returns for Shashi. Rishi says:
'As with all the Kapoors, Shashi Uncle didn't get much. He
should have made a lot more. But the money got siphoned off here
and there.' Kunal agrees. 'My father was basically conned. You can
hide and fudge the accounts if a film is semi-successful, but with a
super-hit, how much can you hide?'

Shashi's failure to make money on *Bobby* was also linked to the
era he did business in—pre-dating the Internet and video piracy.
Big-budget Hindi films were sometimes released in stages across
India, with distributors screening them, region-wise, over a period
of time—somewhat akin to platform releases of art-house films in
the US. So, *Bobby* first opened in Bombay, Haryana and Punjab,
and later in Shashi's territories, Delhi and UP. On witnessing
Bobby's instant connect with the masses, distributors in Haryana
and Punjab took full advantage of the fact that Shashi was yet to
release the film in the capital. They decided to expand their
market by sending busloads of filmgoers from Delhi to the
neighbouring states. '*Dilli sey bhar, bhar ke buses jatee thee Gurgaon
and Faridabad!*' ('Buses would be jam-packed [with moviegoers]
from Delhi to Gurgaon and Faridabad!') Rishi says—so much so
that by the time the actor came to Delhi for the film's premiere,
many people had already watched *Bobby*!

But Shashi was not one to give up after a few setbacks. The real
businessman in him came to the fore, once more, with the iconic
Junoon[7] (more in a bit). Soon after, in 1976, Shashi formed his
company, Film-Valas—clearly inspired by the title of the
Merchant–Ivory film he acted in, *Shakespeare Wallah*. Film-Valas
would go on to produce some of the best-known art-house films
of the late 1970s and 1980s. 'Dad was getting a bit frustrated with
the kind of cinema he was working for,' Kunal says, while
acknowledging that Shashi was making good money as a Hindi
movie actor. Film-Valas and its productions, then, satisfied Shashi's
creative hunger.

Junoon (1978)

In the late 1970s, Shyam Benegal became the leading figure of India's new wave, or the parallel cinema movement, with each of his narrative features—*Ankur*,[8] *Nishant*,[9] *Manthan*[10] and *Bhumika*[11] —earning artistic and box office success for their commitment to realism and their rejection of the song-and-dance extravagance of mainstream Hindi cinema. *Ankur*, for instance, explores—without any overt romanticization—such fraught subjects as caste, women's rights and economic disparity, by recounting the story of Lakshmi, a young peasant woman; as for *Nishant*, it starkly and with startling rawness, studies the tyranny of the feudal system in an India at the cusp of Independence.

Shashi Kapoor keenly followed Shyam's films, and when Film-Valas was born, he asked the director if he had a subject or a story in mind for his first production. 'I jumped at the idea,' Shyam tells me. Having read Ruskin Bond's novella, *A Flight of Pigeons*,[12] Shyam proceeded to tell Shashi a tale set in Shahjahanpur, during the 1857 Indian mutiny—of a married Pathan, Javed Khan, so enamoured by a young Anglo-Indian woman, Ruth, that he kidnaps her family and her, hoping to marry the young lady. Shyam says, 'Shashi just loved the story and announced, "Yes, we will make it!" And that was it.'

A Flight of Pigeons was fleshed out to create a script for *Junoon*— written by Shyam himself, with dialogues by Satyadev Dubey and Ismat Chughtai. So compelling was the screenplay that Shashi, who had at first only planned to produce the film, now tendered a request to Shyam. 'After reading the script, I asked Shyam if he wanted me to act in the film,' Shashi tells Madhu Jain.[13]

For Shyam, the decision was easy. Having worked with relatively unknown theatre actors, or with fresh talent from the National School of Drama and/or the Film and Television Institute of India, he was only too excited to have a big name attached to his project. Shyam offered the lead role of Javed Khan to Shashi.

Shashi, on his part, was not the clichéd egoist one would expect a movie hero to be, but a team player. 'He was extremely diligent,' Shyam asserts. 'He never for once played the star—although at that time he was a *huge* star. He worked with the discipline of a theatre actor. You know, actors in a repertory theatre company—how disciplined they have to be. You give them a certain time, and they are always ready to go in front of the camera on schedule—make-up done, costume worn. That was Shashi Kapoor, my actor.'

While Nafisa Ali (a national swimming champion and a Miss India) played Ruth, Shyam was convinced that the role of Ruth's unrelenting mother, Miriam, who uses a potent combination of vehemence and guile to fight Javed, had to be offered to Jennifer Kendal Kapoor—who had not appeared before a camera for nearly a decade since *Bombay Talkie*. 'Jennifer was very nervous in the beginning,' Shyam says. 'She even asked, "Can't you get someone else?" But once she appeared in front of the camera, all her hesitancy vanished.'

Junoon has terrific performances across the board, but the best moments in the film are between Jennifer/Miriam and Shashi/Javed as they argue over his desire to marry Ruth. In a particularly gripping moment, Miriam, taking advantage of the ongoing sepoy mutiny and Javed's faith in the rebels, cleverly bargains with her captor. If Delhi falls to the mutineers, Javed can marry Ruth. Then, she adds: '*Agar Angrezon ka kabza ho gaya Dilli par, to phir aap na to Ruth se baat karne ki koshish karenge, na shadi ke liye dabav dalenge. Manzoor?*' ('If the British capture Delhi, you will not try talking to Ruth, nor will you put any pressure on her to marry you. Agreed?') Javed stares at Miriam, aghast, even as he ponders over the ramifications of the deal.

Later, Jennifer's father, Geoffrey Kendal, will be full of praise for his daughter's dialogue-delivery in the film. 'Jennifer started to learn Hindi only after she was married,' he writes in his autobiography, 'and to [watch her] play a long part in *Junoon* with apparent ease was staggering.'[14]

1978, *Junoon*. Shashi Kapoor, as a 1987 mutineer. Here, towards the end of the film, he desperately searches for the Anglo-Indian, Ruth (Nafisa Ali). Courtesy: Shyam Benegal.

Interestingly, Jennifer, much like Shashi, had two roles to perform when the film was being made—she was not just a lead actress, but also, as would often happen, in charge of designing the costumes. Sanjna Kapoor vividly remembers a time when *Junoon* was in the pre-production phase. 'Back then, our house had turned into a tailoring shop,' she says. 'While Mom designed the Western costumes, she personally stitched all the bonnets.' Perhaps because of Jennifer's keen eye for detail, one of the most remarkable aspects of *Junoon* is the get-up of the British and the Indian characters, right down to the extras. 'They were so right and authentic,' Shyam says. 'It was rare for a film, made in India, to bring a period to life with costumes.' Later, in November 1983,

when Om Puri would find himself short of funds while staging
Majma Theatre's hit production, *Bichchoo*, for the first Prithvi
Theatre Festival, Jennifer would take him to Film-Valas' storage
room, pull out all the trunks and give him costumes from *Junoon*
for the play.

Apart from Shashi, Nafisa and Jennifer, *Junoon*'s large ensemble
cast includes Shabana Azmi (as Javed's wife), Naseeruddin Shah
(as Javed's brother-in-law), and Ismat Chugtai (as Miriam's
mother). Shot in the vast expanses of Malihabad and Kakori near
Lucknow, the film also comes with elaborate battle scenes featuring
a massive team of background artists, horses and elephants—with
the crucial exodus towards the end introducing nearly 3,000 extras,
300 animals, 40 horse carriages and bullock carts.

Not surprisingly, *Junoon* proved to be the most expensive film
Shyam had directed until that point. 'It was a very big film for me,'
the director says. 'Not as big as a Rajesh Khanna movie, of course.
But big in comparison to the films I was otherwise making at that
time for 8–10 lakh rupees.' Kunal Kapoor states that *Junoon* cost
Rs 34 lakh, while director and writer Sangeeta Datta quotes a
much higher figure of 'Rs 55 lakh'.[15]

This brings us to Shashi, the producer, and Shyam is quick to
inform me, 'I have never had a better producer than him!' He adds,
'Shashi wasn't just sitting there, putting money and being critical.
He did much more than that. He participated in the whole
process. He saw things from the point of view of a filmmaker and
an insider. He didn't require any interpretation. He understood
what was essential. There are very few producers of that kind—
you can literally count them on your fingers.'

Shashi, as producer, was always the first to arrive on the set and
the last to leave. Apart from earning quite a reputation for his
discipline, he came to be known for his high ethical standards.
Shyam says, 'I remember, once, someone was lolling around,
smoking a cigarette. Shashi got so angry with him! He said,

"Listen, the set is like a temple. You wouldn't do this on stage, would you? Then don't attempt this kind of thing on a film set!'"

Shabana, who always mock-sparred with Shashi, has a story of her own to share. 'While shooting *Junoon*, I remember, I was waiting for my turn and listening to The Beatles. And Shashi came in screaming, *"Yeh koi sense hai? 1857 ki picture ban rahi hai aur tum Beatles sun rahi ho?"* ("Does this make any sense? We are shooting a film set in 1857 and you are listening to The Beatles?") So, I asked, *"Yeh kya dadagiri hai aapki?"* ("Why are you acting like a local thug?") And he said, *"Begum Akhtar lagao." Maine kaha, "Maaf karna, Begum Akhtar bhi 1857 main nahin thi."* ("Listen to Begum Akhtar." And I said, "Excuse me, Begum Akhtar was not around in 1857 either.")'

For Shabana, Shashi's most remarkable trait as a producer was the respect with which he treated everyone. 'You know, the film industry is a very hierarchical place,' she says. 'And there is a big difference between stars and those playing minor roles. Shashi, perhaps because he comes from the world of theatre, remained sensitive to the needs of all actors, big or small.' It was his democratic temper that made him book the entire cast of *Junoon*—and not just the lead actors—for two months into the Clarks Avadh Hotel in Lucknow. Shabana says, 'These are the quiet little things he paid for which made him very unusual. But it also made him exactly like his father—my mother tells me that Prithviraj Kapoor had immense respect for his workers.' Shashi, in more ways than one, was his father's son.

Despite the spiralling cost of production, *Junoon* eventually broke even or, as Shyam says, 'There was no problem recovering money, but there was a problem when it came to making profits.' He adds, 'People in the film industry would say, "Okay, Shashi and Shyam make art-house films with good performances, but where is the cash ringing?"'

Money, however, cannot be the only meter for success. *Junoon* travelled the world, visiting Moscow, Montreal, Cairo and Sydney, and collected a string of awards. It earned recognition as the best feature film in Hindi in the 1979 National Awards, and swept the Filmfare Awards in 1980, winning best film, director and dialogues.

Kalyug (1981)

Soon after *Junoon*, Shashi Kapoor and Shyam Benegal began charting plans for the future. 'I asked Shashi if he would like to produce a second film, based on an idea that (actor and playwright) Girish Karnad and I had been working on for some time,' Shyam says. 'It was to be a modern rendering of a family feud among cousins—which, in fact, forms the basis of the Mahabharata. Girish had drafted the outline of a script and Shashi agreed to produce it.' That was how *Kalyug*,[16] the second Shashi–Shyam collaboration, which modernized an Indian epic, began.

The cast was almost as large as the Mahabharata, and Shyam brought in a range of young and senior actors, including Raj Babbar, Anant Nag, Sushma Seth, Kulbhushan Kharbanda, Vijaya Mehta, Supriya Pathak and Victor Banerjee, and two big stars— Shashi, who'd play the role of Karan Singh (or Karna of the Kauravas), the advisor and loyalist to the Khubchand clan; and Rekha as Supriya, the Draupadi-like wife of Dharamraj (a character akin to Yudhishthira, played by Raj Babbar), head of the competing Puranchand family. To complicate this interwoven narrative is a subplot involving Supriya, who is secretly in love with her brother-in-law, Bharat (Anant Nag as the modern-day Arjuna). What follows is a tale of violent corporate conflict and familial bloodlust.

Rekha came to be part of *Kalyug* 'because of Shashi actually', Shyam says, reminding me that *Kalyug* would be Shashi's eleventh film with her. Shashi would eventually star in eighteen films with the actress—the highest number he'd accept alongside any Hindi film actor. 'It was a joint decision,' Shyam continues. 'I would have chosen Rekha myself for *Kalyug*, but I don't think she would have worked for me if I had asked her.' Several years later, Shyam would cast Rekha again, this time in the Khalid Mohamed-scripted drama, *Zubeidaa*.[17]

Unlike *Junoon*, Shashi did not volunteer to play Karan in *Kalyug*—while the role was, without a doubt, pivotal to the film's plot, it still had only a supporting function. Instead, Shashi wished to play the lead as Dharamraj, and planned to offer Amitabh Bachchan the part of Karan. 'But it didn't quite work out like that,' Shyam says. 'I could only see Shashi as Karan Singh, and I didn't approach Amitabh. I think Shashi did. But as it turned out at that time, Amitabh was right on top of the heap and had different ambitions and other work.' At one point, Shashi even considered offering the role of Karan to Satyajit Ray's favorite actor, Soumitra Chatterjee. Shashi says that this was about the only time Soumitra came close to working in a Hindi film: '[But] since he was unwell he couldn't accept my offer.'[18]

With his plans falling through, Shashi, without any bitterness, accepted the part of Karan, even conceding, 'Had [Soumitra] performed he would have done more justice to the character than I [could].'[19] Shyam says, 'That was how he was—he was okay sharing space even though he was a big star. Now, there are very few who do that.' Interestingly, despite not being the lead actor, Shashi got top billing in *Kalyug*, followed by Rekha—a function, really, of their star status in the industry.

According to Dev Benegal, who had secured his first film unit job in *Kalyug*, Shashi, upon accepting the role of Karan, 'was an absolutely professional actor. He would get into the skin of the character—almost as though he were on stage. He would be in the wings within an hour of receiving the script and dive into the role.'

There is a crucial scene in *Kalyug*, where Shashi's Karan learns about the identity of his mother—again, bearing a strong resemblance with Karna, who learns, to disastrous consequence, that his mother is Kunti. Karan is so devastated that he takes an embryonic position, curling up in a bed—making this among the greatest scenes shot in a Hindi film and one of the most outstanding collaborations between Shyam and Shashi. 'He worked very hard on it,' Shyam says. Dev adds, 'It was top-angle shot and it took a long time to set up. After the scene was done, Shashi came out and asked if it was okay. We didn't have monitors at that time but I was allowed to stand by the cameras. I told him he was absolutely brilliant and set the mood perfectly. Shashi grinned and said, "Well, you know what I was thinking about?" I was a young, green boy, very quiet and shy—Shashi and his wife were so warm and welcoming as a couple that those inhibitions should have disappeared—still, I looked at him blankly. And Shashi said, "I was thinking, I hope my wife is not making baingan (aubergine) for dinner tonight. I hope there is something else to eat." I just smiled. But that statement stayed in my head.'

The instant when Shashi learns of his mother is one among several remarkable moments in *Kalyug*. Although each character grabs limited screen-time, many have intensely felt scenes—be it Sushma Seth's Savitri, the Puranchand matriarch (or Kunti), who conveys with a great deal of pathos her disapproval of the family feud; or the moment when Victor Banerjee's Dhanraj (or Duryodhana) accepts Karan's resignation. These performance-driven moments; the flashes of intrigue; and the disturbing, erotic ending, quite unlike anything attempted in Hindi cinema prior, make *Kalyug* a notable drama.

Even so, weaving the narrative of Mahabharata into the lives of two contemporary industrial families at war over competing businesses was fraught with challenges. Shyam says, 'I was never satisfied with the way *Kalyug* turned out'; it would be the first time that he would have to compromise when a film failed to take shape as he had intended. Director Sangeeta Datta, while critically analyzing the film, pinpoints the shortcomings: 'Characters [in *Kalyug*] are hurtling around in a sweeping tide of events, so the filmmaker was unable to explore their inner worlds.' Shyam, in turn, admits to Sangeeta, 'There were script problems which did not get untied till the end.'[20]

In fact, Dev—who, among other things, had to take the dialogues written by Shyam's regular scriptwriter, Satyadev Dubey, transcribe them in Devanagari and English, and distribute the dialogue sheets to all the actors—suggests that the lack of a thorough screenplay was the film's undoing. 'There really wasn't a script we were filming or never a script that I saw,' he says. 'I had a file which was a one-page step outline of the film.' Sometimes, the dialogues would be handed over to the actors the night before, but at other times, they would get them on the day of the shoot, while the shot was being set up. Now and again, the dialogues would

1981, *Kalyug*. Shyam Benegal to the left; Govind Nihalani behind the camera; and Shashi Kapoor to his right in a recent avatar as producer. Courtesy: Shyam Benegal.

abruptly change. 'Victor Banerjee really wanted the dialogues ahead of time,' Dev says. 'He was not very comfortable with Hindi. He wanted a while to absorb the language. But he was never able to get the dialogues on schedule. Shashi—while he would be annoyed if his lines would not come in early—would get even more concerned about the other actors.'

This wasn't Shashi's only cause for concern. Dev remembers the star dealing with production crises even while acting in *Kalyug*. 'There was a production set-up which was being run in an improvised or, what I would call, an ad hoc manner,' he says. 'And Shashi was trying to accommodate this style of filmmaking. There was clearly a kind of tension.'

Despite good intentions and some amazing performances, *Kalyug* failed at the box office. Shashi tells Madhu Jain that the film lost Rs 10 lakh.[21]

In 1988, B.R. Chopra produced and directed a 94-episode Doordarshan television serial—a faithful, if over-the-top, retelling of the Mahabharata. The show, with deep religious connotations, was a huge success. In contrast, *Kalyug*, which made an early attempt at finding contemporary meaning in an ancient epic, failed to sit well with the audience.

36 Chowringhee Lane (1981)

Aparna Sen, who started her acting career with Satyajit Ray's 'Samapti', part of the *Teen Kanya*[22] trilogy, went on to work in several Bengali films and then, also, in Hindi commercial cinema. Along the way, she kept writing—first, a short story, which got considerably longer, and finally became an English screenplay—a heartbreaking story about a lonely, old Anglo-Indian schoolteacher in modern-day Calcutta, whose only source of comfort is teaching Shakespeare.

Script in hand, Aparna approached a few potential producers. "'Sex? Violence? What are you trying to sell?" they would ask me,'

Aparna says. 'And I would answer, "A small human tale."'[23] This comeback was of little interest to most producers.

Finally, at the end of her tether, Aparna shared her script with her mentor, Satyajit, who took a couple of months to get back. His response was reassuring—he liked what he read—and he told Aparna she ought to make the film. When the actress mentioned the difficulties she was facing while seeking producers, Satyajit suggested that she approach Shashi Kapoor, since he had just produced *Junoon*. 'In fact, he told me, he had a gut feeling that Shashi would take this on,' Aparna says.

Aparna sent a synopsis to Shashi, who she already knew through *Bombay Talkie*[24] and also the Salim–Javed scripted *Immaan Dharam*.[25] Shashi called her back in a few days. 'He said, "We liked the synopsis very much, but how do we know you will be able to make a good film out of it?" I said, "I don't know how to convince you." So, he said, "Why don't you fly over from Calcutta to Bombay and read the script to us? And if we take you on, we will pay for your fare back."'

That is how Aparna happened to visit Shashi in Bombay. She read the script to the actor, his wife and the director and cinematographer, Govind Nihalani, who was present at the Kapoors' residence. Kunal Kapoor says that after this script-reading session, his parents liked the narrative so much that they wanted Shyam Benegal to direct the film.[26] But Aparna, in the end, managed to convince them that she was ready to become the director of *36 Chowringhee Lane*[27]—referring to the lead character's desolate residence, and curiously, shot in almost the same address: 26 Chowringhee Road.

To begin with, Aparna wanted to work with Govind for the cinematography. But he was busy at that time as the second unit DOP (director of photography) for Richard Attenborough's *Gandhi*[28]—a commitment that would preoccupy him for at least a year. Aparna—after having waited in the wings for what seemed

like an eternity—was impatient to begin filming, and Shashi
sensed her urgency. He went on to recommend a number of
cinematographers, among them the cameraman of *Witness*,[29] Ashok
Mehta—who, across interviews, has referred to Shashi as his best
public relations officer. On watching *Witness*—a beautifully shot
film starring Shashi, that, sadly, never did get released—Aparna
was convinced that she had found the talent she was looking for.
Ashok would be the cinematographer for *36 Chowringhee Lane*. In
a newspaper interview, Aparna says:

> Ashok and I sat and discussed the visual style of the film.
> We consulted paintings, art books, the works. Then Ashok
> asked me to describe the look of my film in one line. I
> said, 'If a rose was pressed inside a book for a long time,
> you know what the colours would be?' Ashok immediately
> understood what I wanted.[30]

Then came the question of casting. Aparna spent a long time
trying to find the ideal candidate for the lead role of the Anglo-
Indian woman, Violet Stoneham. Finally, actor and director, Utpal
Dutt, recommended Jennifer Kendal Kapoor's name. 'I had seen
Jennifer in *Junoon*, yes. But she seemed so elegant. How could she
play sad, old Miss Stoneham? But Utpalda insisted she was a
wonderful, powerful actor. So, I talked to Jennifer, and I was
honest about my inhibitions—that she looked young. Jennifer
said, "Don't worry, I can think crinkles!"' Aparna laughs as she
remembers the conversation. Ultimately, Jennifer had a make-up
artist fix her hair with a bun at the nape of her neck and mailed her
pictures to Aparna. 'When I got them, I realized that she had got
the essence of the character.'

In a casting coup of sorts, Aparna also roped in Geoffrey
Kendal. As Geoffrey writes in his autobiography: 'I was to play the
part of Jennifer's brother [the ageing and ill Eddie], a part that had
been refused to me earlier because they thought I didn't look old

and decrepit enough. Apparently they had changed their mind.'[31] After James Ivory's *Shakespeare Wallah*,[32] with Felicity and Geoffrey (and with Jennifer in a tiny, uncredited role), *this* father-daughter pair would act together in the same film—peculiarly, as brother and sister. 'My grandfather was absolutely wonderful in it,' Sanjna Kapoor says.

And as would often happen in their home productions, Shashi and Jennifer's kids also made brief appearances in *36 Chowringhee Lane*. Sanjna is the young Violet Stoneham in a dream sequence shot in Bombay's Madh Island. And Sanjna's older brother, Karan Kapoor, plays Violet's boyfriend, Davie, who dies in the Second World War.

Finally, there was the cat to cast! Aparna says, 'When Satyajit Ray read the script, he said, "You have written a cat into it. It's all very well to sit in an air-conditioned room and write about a cat, but I am telling you, what you propose is very difficult." He told me that he had tried to work with a cat in *Apur Sansar*[33] and it had run away in a few days.' Even though she was patiently told that cats cannot be trained for films, Aparna remained adamant. Finally, it was Shashi who got her a cat from Madras. In *36 Chowringhee Lane*, the black tabby named Sir Toby Belch—after a character in *Twelfth Night*[34]—remains Miss Stoneham's companion at home.

Shashi and Govind, together, drew the budget for the film. Aparna thinks the original plan was around Rs 16 lakh, but that the budget may have increased to Rs 24 lakh. 'I wouldn't bet on it, though,' she says. 'The thing is, the budget was really never really discussed with me.' Presumably, the fact that Shashi sold an 18-acre plot of land in Shridon village near Panvel, just outside Bombay, to raise money for *36 Chowringhee Lane*, was also never discussed with Aparna. She adds, 'While the producer of my last three films urged me to complete the shoot in certain number of days, Shashi did not even tell me that. All he suggested was that I should try and keep costs low.'

Aparna says that Shashi, the producer, was not known to penny-pinch. 'Shashi was quite extravagant,' she says. 'We wouldn't work on Sundays. Since the shoot was in Calcutta, he would fly in from Bombay, carrying with him Film-Valas' entire lights equipment, and stay in five-star hotels. Then, he'd be extremely generous with food and drinks for the unit boys each weekend— he always kept the team happy.'

Sharmila Tagore adds that Shashi, the producer, was also remarkably hardworking. 'When he was producing *36 Chowringhee Lane*, Shashi, Jennifer and I were going to Calcutta or coming back—it was one of those plane journeys. And Shashi commented that he'd be waking up bleary-eyed, early in the morning, and getting straight to work, because he was committed to making a good film with Aparna.'

If Shashi and Aparna sparred, it was when *36 Chowringhee Lane* was being edited. Since the actor found the director's cut a tad too long, he went on to chop it quite a bit. 'I was unhappy about that and we had a little tiff, a falling-out,' Aparna says. 'But then, I came to accept it. It was all okay, eventually.'

36 Chowringhee Lane is a beautifully told, quiet film on old age and loneliness, while also providing keen insights into the lives of Calcutta's Anglo-Indians. The film was critically appreciated and won many awards, including a BAFTA (British Academy of Film and Television Arts) nomination in 1982 for Jennifer as the best actress in a leading role—perhaps the only time that a heroine in a film produced and directed in India by Indians has received this recognition. Jennifer's co-nominees were Sissy Spacek for *Missing*[35] and Diane Keaton for *Reds*,[36] but they ultimately lost to Katharine Hepburn for *On Golden Pond*.[37] Jennifer was, however, honoured as the best actress in 1982 by the Evening Standard British Film Awards.

Jennifer remained unaffected by such adulation, almost modest. In an interview, she says, 'I don't think my performance [in *36 Chowringhee Lane*] is as good as people say it is. I think because of the long gap between *Bombay Talkie* and *Junoon*, people had forgotten that I've ever acted.' Then, she goes on to praise Aparna:

> *36 Chowringhee Lane* is one of the rare instances in anybody's career that a writer, who's also a director, has created a character that is so complete...there was never any need for me to justify in my mind anything Miss Stoneham did...nothing went against the grain of that character...Maybe because [Aparna] is also an actress, it became that much easier.[38]

Aparna won the 1981 National Award in the best director category, while Ashok was recognized for his cinematography. Then, there was the 1982 Cinemanila International Film Festival in Manila. Satyajit, who had told Aparna that he liked the film, was the head of the jury. 'There were very many important films competing,' Aparna tells me, 'among them *The French Lieutenant's Woman*,[39] Fassbinder's *Lola*[40] and Truffaut's *The Woman Next Door*.[41] In comparison, I was just a newcomer.' Despite such formidable competition, *36 Chowringhee Lane* was awarded the Golden Eagle for best feature film. Later, Aparna asked Satyajit if he had carried the jury's vote and the master director's heartwarming response was that it was a unanimous decision.

In spite of such international acclaim, *36 Chowringhee Lane* fared poorly at the box office. Kunal describes the film as 'suicidal' since it was made in English, while Geoffrey, in his autobiography, writes, 'The story of a lonely Anglo-Indian spinster, whose only joy in life was teaching Shakespeare [to her students] was not one that would necessarily appeal to a wide audience.'[42] In an interview with *The Hindu*, Shashi expresses his frustration with the film's reception. '*36 Chowringhee Lane* was a total loss,' he says. 'I had to pay for the publicity charges and even, at places, had to hire the theatres myself to exhibit it.'[43] Elsewhere, Shashi says that by his count, the film lost at least Rs 24 lakh[44] (which is the figure quoted by Aparna as the budget of the film).

In hindsight, it wasn't Shashi's best business decision to produce a film and then release it himself. But then, he had no other option. This was the era of single-screen theatres in India. The multiplexes, which offered breathing space to independent films, were far into the future. As many have suggested, Shashi, the producer, was ahead of his time.

Vijeta (1982)

Govind Nihalani met Shashi Kapoor at the cusp of the latter's first big break in the early 1960s. The young actor was playing the lead in *Mohabbat Isko Kahete Hain*,[45] while Govind was coming to grips with an early assignment in the film industry. 'I remember those days with tremendous fondness,' Govind tells me. 'Shashi was a young, up-and-coming actor, while I was just an assistant cameraman. But he was always very kind, friendly and warm with me, and this was his approach to all technicians.'

While Govind and Shashi lost contact after the shoot was wrapped up, the master cinematographer continued following the actor's film-graph. Finally, their lives collided again when Shyam Benegal made *Junoon* and *Kalyug*, and roped in both Govind (as cinematographer) and Shashi (as actor/producer). Their association would only grow in strength when Shashi would ask Govind to direct his home production, *Vijeta*,[46] after catching Govind's critically acclaimed *Aakrosh*,[47] the winner of six Filmfare Awards in 1981.

Vijeta's genesis was rather unusual. In the early 1980s, when Shashi was in Delhi for the International Film Festival, he met Air Chief Marshal Dilbagh Singh, who expressed interest in a Hindi film that would celebrate the Indian Air Force (IAF) and also mark its fiftieth anniversary in 1982. Dilbagh, in turn, offered to provide all facilities for the film—sanctioning the shooting of large segments in the Air Force Academy in Hyderabad, and the Air Force Station and the National Defence Academy in Poona. While Shashi would remain the producer and financier, it was the first time that the IAF would be collaborating with a Hindi film production company.

What's more, the IAF wished to see a story that would break the norm. Instead of following Hindi cinema's time-honoured tradition of portraying army pilots as men of war who leave behind pregnant wives or grieving girlfriends, they wanted to see a more contemporaneous narrative, one that showed the institution engaging with modern concerns. Govind says, 'They wanted an educated pilot in a bid to attract young people. They didn't want the typical portrait of the air force—one where husbands go to war and die.'

With this brief, Govind worked with Shyam's dialogue-writing colleague, Satyadev Dubey, and well-known poet, Dilip Chitre, to create an original story. Using Satyadev's acquaintance with a Sikh gentleman and his Maharashtrian wife as a starting point, the team created a compelling family sketch.

Vijeta tells the story of a stern, once-philandering Sikh man, Nihal (Shashi) in a terribly strained relationship with his Maharashtrian spouse, Neelima (Rekha) and his aimless son, Angad (Kunal Kapoor). A demoralized Angad, who seems to drift from failure to failure, even as he tries coping with his dysfunctional family, finally finds his calling when he joins the air force. What follows is Angad's coming-of-age—his growth from a point of ennui to one of self-realization.

Govind had seen Shashi act under Shyam's guidance, so directing him proved to be relatively easy. 'All I had to do was narrate the scene,' Govind says. 'Since Shashi knew, right from the beginning, that we had created characters with grey areas, he was able to capture the nuances on his own. As an actor, he was very,

very bright.' In *Vijeta*, Shashi offers a deeply felt performance, as a
partner caught in an unhappy marriage that is sustained out of
love for a son. *Vijeta*, along with *Junoon* and *Kalyug*, have Shashi,
the actor, in top form; in each of these films, he shows immense
restraint, even as he plays complex, troubled men.

If Nihal's/Shashi's severity forms the backdrop to *Vijeta*, the
film's focal point is Angad. Shashi's son, Kunal, would earn his
first big break in this film, after small appearances in several other
movies. It is believed that Shashi wished to make *Vijeta* to launch
his son's career, but Govind says that there was no coercion, as
such: 'Well, Shashi did not make it a condition. He left it to us and
suggested that if Kunal could play the role, that was fine.'

Over the course of making the film, Kunal proved to be more
than an actor. *Vijeta*—which, even now, feels somewhat long-
winded—had twenty-two minutes edited out by Kunal using
Shashi's Steenbeck machine, with the able guidance of Bhanudas
Divakar (who had also edited *Junoon* and *Kalyug*, and was working
on Shyam's *Mandi*[48] at that time). 'I felt *Vijeta*'s early cut was far
too monotonous and I thought it should be trimmed,' Kunal says.
'I called Dad and showed him the edited version. He liked it.' Of
course, this was done without Govind's full knowledge, and when
the director learnt of the clandestine editing session, he was most
upset! Finally, to placate Govind, twelve minutes were added back
to the final cut.

Shashi, as the financier of *Vijeta*, is remembered warmly by
Govind, who describes him as a rare producer, responsive to a
director's needs. 'He understood that cinema, ultimately, is a
director's medium,' Govind says. 'Directors should be given what
they want.' Shashi's commitment to enabling his director's vision
shone, even when there were financial constraints during *Vijeta*'s
filming. 'Shashi wasn't a very wealthy producer,' Govind says, 'so
funding had to come from somewhere, no? But he never let that
tension reach the director or the unit. No.'

Unfortunately, as was becoming a regular affair with the other films Shashi produced, *Vijeta* lost money—Rs 40 lakh, Shashi tells Madhu Jain.[49] Kunal clearly regrets the failure of *Vijeta*, especially given his strong performance as Angad. In a *Mint* article, he wistfully says, '*Vijeta* would have made money had he [Shashi] been Ismail Merchant or Ekta Kapoor. It struck a chord, but it wasn't marketed well.'[50] It's a critique that would come to be voiced for Shashi's next production, too.

Utsav (1984)

Mrcchakatika (translated as 'The Little Clay Cart'),[51] attributed to Sudraka, is a ten-act play, rich in humour, which—against a backdrop of political upheaval—celebrates passion. Its plot is fairly straightforward—an impoverished Brahmin, Charudatta, falls in love with a moneyed courtesan, Vasantasena, even as she is pursued by the king's brother-in-law, Samsthanaka; Vatsyayana (of *Kamasutra*[52] fame) is the narrator connecting the events, even while extrapolating on the subject he's best acquainted with: sexual pleasure. If *Mrcchakatika* remains a celebrated play, it is because of the wit and freshness it brings to subjects such as sex and desire in ancient India.

Girish Karnad, who had remained in touch with Shashi Kapoor after *Kalyug*, told the actor that he wanted to direct a film based on Sudraka's classic. Roughly fifty years prior, Prithviraj Kapoor had performed in precisely this play as the lead, Charudatta. Now, Girish wished to give the role of the protagonist to Shekhar Suman, in a film titled *Utsav*,[53] which Prithviraj's son, Shashi, would go on to produce. It would be the last of five films Shashi would finance for directors associated with India's art-house cinema.

While Rekha was to play the beauteous Vasantasena, and Amjad Khan was cast as Vatsyayana, Shashi planned to have his friend, Amitabh Bachchan, as the overweight, lecherous

Samsthanaka. However, after getting seriously injured while
shooting Manmohan Desai's *Coolie*,[54] Amitabh had no choice but
to pull out of the film; Shashi was compelled to accept the
supporting role, while playing producer. For the first time—since
the part required it—Shashi put on weight.

Amitabh's accident was just the first of a series of star-crossed
episodes that plagued the production of *Utsav*. The film's set in
Karnataka was destroyed by a cyclone. Then, on the first day of the
shoot, Rekha's house was raided by the income tax department.
Worst of all, the film's budget jumped from Rs 1.2 crore to Rs 2
crore.

Shashi's early financial plans went awry for a number of reasons.
For one, Shashi and Girish—who had high hopes from *Utsav* and
were convinced that the film would be a crossover success, at least
in art-house theatres in the West—chose to shoot simultaneously
in Hindi and English. British artists were employed to dub voices
in English and a great deal of money was spent internationally.

Unfortunately, this cash outflow could not be recovered, since
the English version would never hit the giant screens. 'I don't
think anyone was interested in it,' says Dev Benegal, who used to
hang out on the sets of *Utsav* with Kunal Kapoor in Bombay, and
would later work on the English version of the film during the
post-production phase in London. 'Back then, Indian actors
speaking English just didn't fly out.' Kunal, who plays a secondary
role in *Utsav*, adds, 'At that point, nobody in the international
market was interested in that period in India. The movie was
neither art-house nor commercial. I imagined it to be a Douglas
Fairbanks kind of adventure.'[55]

The other problem was that costs weren't kept in check.
Sharmila Tagore says: 'Throughout the making of *Utsav*, there
was a lot of money getting drained, which hurt me as a friend. For
instance, Shashi would send those who were used to train-travel
by plane.' Dev adds: 'What's worse, the *Utsav* team was exposing

film like water!' The escalating expenses took a definite toll on Shashi, who finally had a showdown with Girish. 'They argued in front of the crew over the usage of film stock,' Dev says. 'It was the only time I noticed Shashi buckling under pressure. Because, otherwise, he was a dream producer. He would just never say no.'

When the Hindi version of *Utsav* was released in India, it fared disastrously. A number of reasons were attributed to its failure. Sanjna Kapoor, while praising her father in *Utsav*—'He was wonderful: debauched and soulful'—suggests that the performances on the whole were uneven. 'There were all these actors from different acting schools Scotch-taped together!'

Dev goes on to say that the tenor of the film was entirely wrong. *Mrcchakatika* is a humorous play that almost always works on stage. But *Utsav*—burdened, as it is, with period details, production design, costumes and jewellery—is just not funny. 'I remember, once, Shashi told me, "The problem with you filmmakers is that you are scared of making comedies, you don't have a sense of humour,"' Dev recalls. '*Utsav*, frankly, wasn't comic enough. Under Girish's direction, it became a dull, straightforward drama without any wit.'

Kunal, on his part, points out that while the film is meant to engage with erotica, it stops short of truly delving into the subject. In one of the early sequences in the film, Vasantasena, after ensnaring Charudatta, is undressed, but the camera, while panning over parts of her body, avoids being transgressive. In another scene, when Vatsyayana plays a peeping Tom in a pleasure house, the audience is offered a fleeting suggestion, no more, of what he sees. Kunal writes, 'I think Girish should have made the film more glamourous and sexy. There was some nudity in the English version. But in the Hindi version, some of the positions that Amjad Khan sees were cut out.'[56]

Critic Sunil Sethi, in his *India Today* review, agrees that these bouts of coyness hurt the film—then goes on to say that *Utsav*'s chief drawback is that it lacks coherence:

Beautifully photographed, richly mounted, painstakingly recreated, [but] no one is quite certain as to what is going on during its two-hour duration. [...] There are far too many subplots, too many characters spouting badly-written dialogues in supposedly chaste Hindi, far too many digressions [...] to really get to the heart of the matter [...] Utsav achieves little, except hope to get into censor trouble. It's a waste, an expensive waste, and it goes the way of all flesh. Into ashes and dust.[57]

Utsav never quite worked for me either. Despite its obvious opulence, the film seemed to lack inner energy. It felt empty and a tad bit pretentious, with affected dialogues.

Regardless of these flaws, Utsav could have fared remarkably well—but for the now-common problem afflicting Shashi's productions—it wasn't marketed efficiently. Kunal says, 'Consider Merchant–Ivory—their films weren't the kinds you'd open the front door to. And yet, there would be a line of distributors standing outside. They pushed their projects, even after the success of Oscar-nominated films like A Room with a View.[58] Dad was not pushing. Ismail was a hustler. Dad was not.'

Utsav nearly lost Rs 1.5 crore. Kunal writes that this was an especially difficult time for the family, 'Dad was financially wiped out by Utsav. Instead of filling our coffers, it worked us into a completely negative zone.'[59] To make ends meet, Kunal opened an advertising agency, and his brother, Karan Kapoor, who was modelling by then, was involved. Their earnings helped the family tide over a period when they were truly strapped for funds.

It was during this especially trying time that Jennifer Kendal Kapoor was unwell, receiving cancer treatment in London. Shashi tells Madhu Jain, 'Jennifer told me then, "Let's shut shop."'[60]

But instead of closing his production house, Shashi made one last attempt, this time directing a film himself—a massive, extremely expensive cinematic fantasy, styled after *The Arabian Nights*[61] and Hollywood superhero flicks. *Ajooba*[62] would be Shashi's swan song as a producer.

Ajooba (1991)

Ajooba was born when Kunal Kapoor took a trip to Moscow to promote *Utsav*. There, he met an Indian man—one of his father's business friends—who recommended an Indo-Soviet co-production, in the hope that the risks would spread out. It was an idea that appealed to Shashi Kapoor, who had burnt his fingers once too often already. He decided to direct a film with a Soviet co-director, Gennadi Vasilyev, and produce it with the help of Soviet financiers. Given the Soviet connection, it was also determined that much of the shooting would be done in the Soviet Union, including in Yalta by the Black Sea, with local artists playing extras.

What emerged was *Ajooba*, a film unravelling the story of a masked Zorro-like legend—the protector of the people of the kingdom of 'Baharistan', and the destroyer of an evil, devil-worshipping Vazir. This time, Shashi managed to convince his friend and superstar, Amitabh Bachchan, to play the title role. Dimple Kapadia, Rishi Kapoor, Amrish Puri and Shammi Kapoor became part of the supporting cast.

After the actors were signed on, filming began full throttle. Rishi says, 'Shashi Uncle would direct with a stick in his hand. *Maje ke liye*. (Just for fun.)' This is a tale that Amitabh corroborates: 'The story about the stick he carried to the set is actually correct. It was used to maintain discipline and order—more a friendly equipment than anything else.' Amitabh adds that Shashi's direction-with-a-stick act only lasted during the film's shoot in Bombay. 'He lost the baton in Russia. Thank god!'

After a jaunty beginning, though, *Ajooba* ran into serious trouble. Kunal claims that the signs of a financial disaster were there all the time. During a couple of recce trips to the Soviet Union, he noticed that the costs were getting to be perilously high. 'I insisted that Dad meet Daboo (Randhir Kapoor),' Kunal says. 'Daboo and he are very close and Daboo is known to call a spade a spade. He is unbiased. When I told Dad that we were already over-budget and should cancel the film, Daboo agreed with me. But Dad said a firm no. And he went ahead with *Ajooba*.'

While Kunal sensed a looming monetary crisis, Sanjna Kapoor, early on, saw that the film just wasn't developing well. 'I went to Russia for the shoot—it was a tradition that we would play extras. I remember Papa describing a scene to me involving Chintu (her cousin, Rishi) on the back of a donkey. It was beautiful, the way he explained it. But when I saw it, it was just one long midday shot to avoid lighting. It was horrible,' she laughs. 'Really, it was appalling. Papa, he's not a director.'

Worse, in the days to come, everything that could go wrong with the production did. Towards the end of the shoot, as the Soviet Union and its economy began falling apart, the financiers withdrew. There were still a few weeks of shooting to go, and huge parts of the special effects were pending. Shashi, in a bid to complete the film, had to pay for everything from his own pocket.

Ajooba was not the success that Shashi had hoped it would be. It failed miserably at the Indian box office and Shashi suffered a whopping loss of nearly Rs 3.5 crore. If anyone recovered any money, it was Amitabh, who secured distribution rights for Delhi and UP and managed to get an audience.

Critics, on their part, panned *Ajooba*—attacking it for its slapdash special effects, poor performances and the many inconsistencies in plot. Even those involved with the film could not get around to defending it. Rishi, who is never one to mince words, says: '*Ajooba* was absolutely rubbish!' Sanjna adds: 'Dad decided he would direct *Ajooba* and make money with all the stars. But it shows you that stars do not necessarily make a film. It has to be a *good* movie.' Kunal has the final word in his article in *Mint*: '*Ajooba* wasn't and isn't a good film. We didn't let Dad make another one after that.'[63]

When I watched *Ajooba* at the time of its release, it was hard to tell if it was meant to be a children's fantasy tale or an action adventure drama for adults. Now, the film feels terribly dated, almost an embarrassment. Yet over the years, *Ajooba* has gained cult status. Some fans claim it is so-bad-it's-good—Madhu Jain being one of them, when she writes in a review:

> [*Ajooba*] takes you for a bit of a ride. But once the willing suspension of disbelief is in place, it should appeal to children and to the child-in-man. Shashi isn't staking a claim to big brother Raj's mantle in his directorial debut—'I can't ever step into his shoes. He was a great filmmaker.' But traces of the showman are there. The Soviet dalliance. The belief in entertainment. 'My interest is all for your delight,' he says, quoting the bard. [...] Most critics have raised their brows on *Ajooba*. But send logic on a holiday have some is good escapist fare.[64]

*

The question that is often raised is whether Shashi Kapoor was a good producer. There are those—especially the directors he hired—who endlessly talk about how generous he was. Madhu Jain, not just a critic and a journalist but also Shashi's friend, echoes these sentiments: 'I think Shashi was a real showman because he did everything *dil se* (from his heart). For *Bobby*,[65] he threw a big party, gave radios to each technician and then took care of everybody on the set, not just the stars. Shashi was a lot like his dad—you see, both, in their childhoods, got khana that was leftover.'

Shashi's children, too, have memories of their father's open-handedness. While Kunal Kapoor remembers the lavish donga parties his father threw for *Jab Jab Phool Khile*,[66] Sanjna Kapoor recollects visiting Raffles Hotel, the legendary five-star in Singapore, with her father soon after he had shot one of his early British productions, *Pretty Polly*.[67] 'When *Pretty Polly* happened, he was going through a slump. Yet, he threw his usual elaborate party for the crew in this wonderful hotel.'

That Shashi's kindness never waned, even when he was in the midst of financial woes, is further emphasized by Sharmila Tagore, who says, 'He was so generous and so good. Even when he was finally bankrupt, he returned each and every person's principal money.'

Naturally, Shashi was adored by actors, film crew and directors for his benevolence. Sanjna says: 'I remember Supriya Pathak telling me, "Oh, Shashi Kapoor was the best producer because he took all of us to Lucknow and put us in the Clarks Avadh during the making of *Junoon*. He said we could order anything we wanted. So we would have vanilla ice cream with hot chocolate sauce for breakfast, lunch and dinner." That's what she told me.'

Yet, Shashi's big-heartedness wasn't necessarily an asset, and his children are candid about this. Sanjna says: 'The thing is, Papa would be extravagant to the extent of being foolish. Because he had experienced life on "the other side", he would give directors whatever they asked for, as much as he possibly could. And that wasn't always wise. Directors also need to be controlled. But Papa was hopeless at that. He spent a lot money on pretty much everything.'

What we see emerging is a fairly complex portrait—Shashi was undoubtedly a director's/actor's producer. But this did not make him a *good* producer. His son, Kunal, agrees: 'My dad was a bad businessman. Even in a film like *Junoon* where he should have made money—it was his own company—he hardly made anything.' Elsewhere, he writes, even more vehemently, 'My dad was the world's worst producer! He never said no [...] He wasn't doing it for the money. He wouldn't even know how much money he had in his pocket.'[68]

Yet, surely, this made Shashi a rare financier—one who held on to his ideals and risked backing the cinema he loved, despite being involved with the business of filmmaking. Dev Benegal tells me that Shashi was the only producer who was using his own money, or what he borrowed, to fund new, art-house films in India. The others, who were part of India's new wave, parallel cinema movement in the 1970s and 1980s, were funded by the government-run FFC—later known as the NFDC (National Film Development Corporation). 'The films Shashi produced were passion projects—he'd take on directors who were not commercial and fund them to make their films,' Dev says. 'It pre-dates what The Weinstein Company or Sony Pictures Classics now do or what David Putnam was attempting in England.'

Yet, Govind Nihalani tells me that it is precisely this childlike zeal for filmmaking that interfered with Shashi's ability to make judicious decisions: 'He would get carried away by the art or the creative part of producing films. Over time, people began saying, "*Shashiji bade dilwale hain, bahut alag kisam ki filmein banate hain.*" ("Shashiji has a big heart. He makes unusual films.") But then, they'd add, he should be careful about the deals he signs with financiers. I would hear things like, "*Shashiji business main zyada dhayan dette to aur bhi achcha hota.*" ("It would be great if Shashiji could have paid more attention to business.") It was a polite way of saying that people took advantage of his goodness.'

Dev agrees with this assessment: 'Shashi took on guys, trusted them, threw money and gave them carte blanche. They had an open chequebook and could do whatever they liked. In many ways, I think they betrayed that trust.' It is something Sharmila comments on, too: 'Shashi treated everybody equally and introduced professionalism but, of course, no one appreciated that in India.'

It took Shashi a while to wisen up to such let-downs. Anil

Dharker says, 'I remember Shashi telling me one day about a director—I won't mention his name, but he was part of a film that Shashi had produced. He said, *"Jab FFC ke liye film banate hain* (when they make films for FFC), directors work with a small budget. *Lekin ab Shashi Kapoor producer ban gaya* (but the moment Shashi Kapoor is producer), they suddenly loosen the purse strings and have no control over expenses!" It was a rare show of bitterness.'

Like so many others who love Shashi, the human being, Anil maintains that Shashi, the film businessman, was a failure—'He had a big heart and a healthy dose of good intentions in his system. But his spirit of generosity prevailed over the kind of discipline a producer should have on the budget.'

One can't help but ask: would the fate of Shashi's films have been different had he been a more circumspect producer? Would they have been box office successes? Possibly not—given that each of them was treading new ground. But at the very least, they would not have been mighty commercial failures. Anil, though, remains a voice of optimism: 'Why, if Shashi's films had been made with a tight budget, I actually think they would have made a profit!'

Today, all is conjecture.

Notes

1. Quoted in Madhu Jain, *The Kapoors: The First Family of Indian Cinema* (New Delhi: Penguin, 2005), p. 247.
2. 1970, *Bombay Talkie*, dir. James Ivory, prod. Ismail Merchant, starring Shashi Kapoor, Jennifer Kendal, Zia Mohyeddin.
3. 1969, *A Thousand and One Nights*, dir. Eiichi Yamamoto, prod. Osamu Tezuka, starring (as voice-overs) Yukio Aoshima, Kyoko Kishida, Hiroshi Akutagawa.
4. 1973, *Bobby*, dir. Raj Kapoor, prod. Raj Kapoor, starring Rishi Kapoor, Dimple Kapadia, Prem Nath.
5. 1978, *Satyam Shivam Sundaram*, dir. Raj Kapoor, prod. Raj Kapoor, starring Shashi Kapoor, Zeenat Aman, Padmini Kolhapure.

6. 1970, *Mera Naam Joker*, dir. Raj Kapoor, prod. Raj Kapoor, starring Raj Kapoor, Simi Garewal, Manoj Kumar.
7. 1978, *Junoon*, dir. Shyam Benegal, prod. Shashi Kapoor, starring Shashi Kapoor, Shabana Azmi, Jennifer Kendal.
8. 1974, *Ankur*, dir. Shyam Benegal, prod. Mohan J. Bijlani, Freni Variava, starring Shabana Azmi, Anant Nag, Sadhu Meher.
9. 1975, *Nishant*, dir. Shyam Benegal, prod. Mohan J. Bijlani, Freni Variava, starring Shabana Azmi, Naseeruddin Shah, Girish Karnad.
10. 1976, *Manthan*, dir. Shyam Benegal, prod. Gujarat Co-operative Milk Marketing Federation Ltd and Sahyadri Films, starring Smita Patil, Girish Karnad, Naseeruddin Shah.
11. 1977, *Bhumika*, dir. Shyam Benegal, prod. Lalit M. Bijlani, Freni Variava, starring Smita Patil, Amol Palekar, Anant Nag.
12. Ruskin Bond, *A Flight of Pigeons* (New Delhi: Penguin, 2007).
13. Madhu Jain, *The Kapoors: The First Family of Indian Cinema* (New Delhi: Penguin, 2005), p. 247.
14. Geoffrey Kendal, *The Shakespeare Wallah: An Autobiography* (London: Sidgwick & Jackson, 1986), p. 174.
15. Sangeeta Datta, *Shyam Benegal* (London: British Film Institute, 2002), p. 120.
16. 1981, *Kalyug*, dir. Shyam Benegal, prod. Shashi Kapoor, starring Shashi Kapoor, Rekha, Raj Babbar.
17. 2001, *Zubeidaa*, dir. Shyam Benegal, prod. Farouq Rattonsey, starring Karisma Kapoor, Rekha, Manoj Bajpai.
18. Quoted in Priyanka Dasgupta, 'Why B'wood Didn't Cast Soumitra Chatterjee,' *The Times of India*, 23 March 2012.
19. *Ibid.*
20. Sangeeta Datta, *Shyam Benegal* (London: British Film Institute, 2002), pp. 128–29.
21. Madhu Jain, *The Kapoors: The First Family of Indian Cinema* (New Delhi: Penguin, 2005), p. 248.
22. 1961, 'Samapti', *Teen Kanya*, dir. Satyajit Ray, prod. Satyajit Ray, starring Soumitra Chatterjee, Aparna Sen, Sita Mukherjee.
23. Quoted in 'Sen in the City', *The Hindu*, 5 July 2004.
24. 1970, *Bombay Talkie*, dir. James Ivory, prod. Ismail Merchant, starring Shashi Kapoor, Jennifer Kendal, Zia Mohyeddin.
25. 1977, *Immaan Dharam*, dir. Desh Mukherjee, prod. Premji, starring Amitabh Bachchan, Shashi Kapoor, Sanjeev Kumar, Rekha.
26. Kunal Kapoor, 'Shashi Kapoor', *Mint*, 4 May 2013.

27. 1981, *36 Chowringhee Lane*, dir. Aparna Sen, prod. Shashi Kapoor, starring Jennifer Kendal, Debashree Roy, Dhritiman Chatterjee.

28. 1982, *Gandhi*, dir. Richard Attenborough, prod. Richard Attenborough, starring Ben Kingsley, Rohini Hattangadi, Roshan Seth.

29. 1974, *Witness*, dir. Raj Marbros, starring Shashi Kapoor, Raakhee, Utpal Dutt.

30. Subhash K. Jha, 'Aparna Sen Devastated by Ashok Mehta's Death', *The Times of India*, 27 August 2012.

31. Geoffrey Kendal, *The Shakespeare Wallah: An Autobiography* (London: Sidgwick & Jackson, 1986), p. 169.

32. 1965, *Shakespeare Wallah*, dir. James Ivory, prod. Ismail Merchant, starring Shashi Kapoor, Felicity Kendal, Madhur Jaffrey.

33. 1959, *Apur Sansar*, dir. Satyajit Ray, prod. Satyajit Ray, starring Soumitra Chatterjee, Sharmila Tagore, Alok Chakravarty.

34. William Shakespeare, *Twelfth Night* (London: Wordsworth, 1995).

35. 1982, *Missing*, dir. Costa-Gavras, prod. Edward Lewis, Mildred Lewis, Peter Guber, Jon Peters, starring Jack Lemmon, Sissy Spacek, Melanie Mayron.

36. 1981, *Reds*, dir. Warren Beatty, prod. Warren Beatty, starring Warren Beatty, Diane Keaton, Edward Herrmann.

37. 1981, *On Golden Pond*, dir. Mark Rydell, prod. Bruce Gilbert, starring Katharine Hepburn, Henry Fonda, Jane Fonda.

38. Quoted in Surender Bhatia, 'Jennifer Kapoor is Back from Our Archives to Talk about Being in the Kapoor Khandaan', *Society*, 7 June 2013.

39. 1981, *The French Lieutenant's Woman*, dir. Karel Reisz, prod. Leon Clore, starring Meryl Streep, Jeremy Irons, David Warner.

40. 1981, *Lola*, dir. Rainer Werner Fassbinder, prod. Wolf-Dietrich Brücker, Horst Wendlandt, starring Barbara Sukowa, Armin Mueller-Stahl, Mario Adorf.

41. 1981, *The Woman Next Door*, dir. François Truffaut, prod. François Truffaut, starring Fanny Ardant, Gérard Depardieu, Henri Garcin.

42. Geoffrey Kendal, *The Shakespeare Wallah: An Autobiography* (London: Sidgwick & Jackson, 1986), p. 169.

43. Quoted in 'A New Role for Shashi Kapoor', *The Hindu*, 11 December 2004.

44. Quoted in Madhu Jain, *The Kapoors: The First Family of Indian Cinema* (New Delhi: Penguin, 2005), p. 248.

45. 1965, *Mohabbat Isko Kahete Hain*, dir. Akhtar Mirza, starring Nanda, Shashi Kapoor, Ramesh Deo.

46. 1982, *Vijeta*, dir. Govind Nihalani, prod. Shashi Kapoor, starring Shashi Kapoor, Rekha, Kunal Kapoor.

47. 1980, *Aakrosh*, dir. Govind Nihalani, prod. Devi Dutt, Narayan Kenny, starring Naseeruddin Shah, Smita Patil, Om Puri.

48. 1983, *Mandi*, dir. Shyam Benegal, prod. Lalit M. Bijlani, Freni Variava, starring Shabana Azmi, Smita Patil, Naseeruddin Shah.

49. Madhu Jain, *The Kapoors: The First Family of Indian Cinema* (New Delhi: Penguin, 2005), p. 248.

50. Kunal Kapoor, 'Shashi Kapoor', *Mint*, 4 May 2013.

51. Sudraka, *Mrcchakatika*, translated by Arthur Llewellyn Basham, Arvind Sharma (New York: State University of New York Press, 1994).

52. Vatsyayana, *Kamasutra*, translated by Richard Burton (New York: Dover, 2006).

53. 1984, *Utsav*, dir. Girish Karnad, prod. Shashi Kapoor, starring Shekhar Suman, Rekha, Shashi Kapoor.

54. 1983, *Coolie*, dir. Manmohan Desai, prod. Ketan Desai, starring Amitabh Bachchan, Rishi Kapoor, Rati Agnihotri.

55. Kunal Kapoor, 'Shashi Kapoor', *Mint*, 4 May 2013.

56. *Ibid.*

57. Sunil Sethi, 'The Way of All Flesh', *India Today*, 15 May 1984.

58. 1985, *A Room with a View*, dir. James Ivory, prod. Ismail Merchant, starring Maggie Smith, Helena Bonham Carter, Denholm Elliott.

59. Kunal Kapoor, 'Shashi Kapoor', *Mint*, 4 May 2013.

60. Madhu Jain, *The Kapoors: The First Family of Indian Cinema* (New Delhi: Penguin, 2005), p. 248.

61. *The Arabian Nights*, translated by Husain Haddawy, Ed. Muhsin Mahdi (New York: Norton, 1990).

62. 1991, *Ajooba*, dir. Shashi Kapoor, prod. Shashi Kapoor, starring Amitabh Bachchan, Rishi Kapoor, Dimple Kapadia.

63. Kunal Kapoor, 'Shashi Kapoor', *Mint*, 4 May 2013.

64. Madhu Jain, 'Fantastic Fare', *India Today*, 15 May 1991.

65. 1973, *Bobby*, dir. Raj Kapoor, prod. Raj Kapoor, starring Rishi Kapoor, Dimple Kapadia, Prem Nath.

66. 1965, *Jab Jab Phool Khile*, dir. Suraj Prakash, prod. Chetan K., starring Shashi Kapoor, Nanda, Agha.

67. 1967, *Pretty Polly*, dir. Guy Green, prod. George W. George, Frank Granat, starring Hayley Mills, Shashi Kapoor, Trevor Howard.

68. Kunal Kapoor, 'Shashi Kapoor', *Mint*, 4 May 2013.

6

THE LATTER-DAY FILMS
Shashi, the 1980s and Beyond

In the early 1980s, Ramesh Sharma—a young director who had won a National Award (best information film, 1978) for *Rumtek*,[1] a short documentary on Tibetan Buddhism—wished to break new ground with a narrative feature. Coming, as he did, from a fairly journalistic background, he considered a story inspired by the investigative reportage being pursued by the likes of Arun Shourie and M.J. Akbar after the Emergency. 'There was an anti-establishment impetus,' he tells me. 'The prevailing mood was that the government was trying to hide something.' So, Ramesh started writing a script, and then, most unexpectedly, met the legendary poet, Gulzar, through a common friend. 'Gulzar loved the outline of the story I was working on and agreed to come on board as the scriptwriter for practically peanuts,' Ramesh says.

Just as serendipitously, Ramesh met a wealthy college friend at the Delhi airport who, after a brief conversation, agreed to fund the director's small indie film which came with a price tag of Rs 25 lakh. But the friend had one condition. He wanted a big commercial actor to play the lead role.

This posed a problem for Ramesh who was planning to cast

niche actors like Om Puri or Naseeruddin Shah—both at the peak of their careers in the art-house, new wave cinema circuit. Ramesh confided in his friend and cameraman, Subrata Mitra (the two had collaborated for *Rumtek*), who cryptically told the young filmmaker that there was a potential star who could play the lead role. A day later, Subrata revealed the name of the actor he had been considering—Shashi Kapoor.

Since Subrata had worked with Shashi on a few Merchant–Ivory films, the cinematographer was aware of the actor's commitment to small, true-to-life movies; he also knew that Shashi had the capacity to shine while portraying layered characters. Ramesh recalls, 'Then, Subrata said, "It's up to you to convince Shashi Kapoor."'

New Delhi Times (1986)

It was 1983. Ramesh Sharma was ready to take a shot in the dark—approach Shashi Kapoor to play the lead in his film titled *New Delhi Times*.[2] The movie planned to explore the story of an upright newspaper editor, Vikas Pande, who sets out to investigate a statesman's assassination. Ramesh says, 'I flew to Bombay—a very, very nervous man. This was my first feature film; I was young, practically out of college, and I had no idea what I would tell this "star" called Shashi Kapoor.'

An anxious Ramesh met Shashi for dinner at the Golden Dragon restaurant in the Taj Mahal Hotel. All of a sudden, halfway through Ramesh's conversation with him, Shashi approached the Hindi film actor, Jeetendra, seated at the next table with some friends. Ramesh says, 'Shashi introduced me as the director of his next film. I was flabbergasted because I had just started narrating the story! But then, I was also happy.'

A now-buoyant Ramesh went on to reveal the rest of the film's plot to Shashi—of journalist Vikas Pande's detection of a much larger political conspiracy while trailing the statesman's assassination; his struggle to ensure that his exposé wasn't quashed; and his later discovery of the slimy nexus between politicians and media barons. 'Shashi loved the story,' Ramesh tells me. 'Really, Shashi was a darling. He treated me like a professional and an equal, as if I had made a dozen films.'

But then, there came the pivotal question. Ramesh says, 'Shashi asked me what the budget for the film was. I bit my tongue and muttered, "Rs 25 lakh." Shashi looked at me, aghast, and finally asked, "Ramesh, are you serious?" I told him that it was all I had and that everyone was working for practically no salary.' Shashi subsided into silence. Then, he asked the young director how much money he had in his pocket. 'I told him I had a couple of thousands. Shashi said, "Give me one hundred and one rupees." I was quite confused. Then, he added, "This is my signing amount. Today is jumma—an auspicious day—and you have signed me on." That was it. He hadn't even read the script.'

It was now time to discuss the star's salary. But by this stage, Shashi was so intrigued by the project that he voluntarily chose to work for merely one lakh rupees—the same amount B.R. Chopra had paid him almost two decades earlier for *Waqt*.[3] However, in return, Shashi posed two conditions (which came to be met). Ramesh remembers the first stipulation: 'Shashi said, "I normally don't do this and you will keep the terms of payment to yourself; do not tell any other director or producer because they will assume I am desperate for work."' Then came the second condition. Ramesh says, 'He wanted to stay at Delhi's Taj Mansingh Hotel. He offered to pay for his own food, drinks and telephone calls, but the location was non-negotiable. He told me, "When people meet me, they should know that Shashi Kapoor's standards haven't entirely dropped."' Later, there was also talk of a third proviso—that Shashi would get a back-end share of 5 per cent from the film.

What made Shashi accept Ramesh's movie? In an interview with *The New York Times*' Lawrence Van Gelder, Shashi hints at the rationale guiding his decision: 'I have not done many politically motivated films,' he says, while describing *New Delhi Times* as a Watergate-like movie in the world of investigative journalism.[4]

With Shashi on board, Sharmila Tagore was signed on to play Nisha, a successful lawyer and the protagonist's wife. It was also decided that the film would be shot in Delhi in July and August 1984. But the plan got derailed more than once.

To begin with, Shashi found himself in the middle of a terrible personal crisis. Ramesh got a desperate call from the star one day. Jennifer was unwell, he said, battling cancer in London; he could not leave her side. 'He kept begging, saying he couldn't do the film,' Ramesh remembers, 'but I told him I would wait for him.' Jennifer passed away in early September 1984.

Soon after, there came a national catastrophe. Indira Gandhi was assassinated and the capital began reeling under anti-Sikh riots. 'Delhi was a complete mess,' Ramesh says, 'and we had to postpone the film yet again. But, at least, this gave Shashi some time to recover. As we'd later learn, he'd never fully mend—but, by the bye, he was in a position to meet people.'

Eventually, shooting began in January 1985, and the location was shifted from Delhi to Film City in Bombay. In hindsight, Ramesh thinks his decision to wait it out was wise, particularly since it meant that he could work with Shashi. 'He was a professional to the core,' Ramesh says. 'He would always come on time. His lines would be ready. And he was, for the most part, a one-take actor—very instinctive. I had no problem with that man!' It was Ramesh's decision to give Shashi a moustache in the film. 'He was a handsome guy and I didn't want his looks to distract viewers from his character. Also, I felt that the moustache would grant him intellectual gravitas.'

New Delhi Times proved to be a taut political thriller with finely-etched characters, and a rare plot that considered loaded subjects like journalistic objectivity and media corruption. But the film ran into all kinds of trouble. There was a lawsuit filed against

1986, *New Delhi Times*. Shashi Kapoor plays the role of Vikas Pande, an upright journalist. Courtesy: Ramesh Sharma.

1986, *New Delhi Times*. Shashi Kapoor, as the busy journalist Vikas Pande, talks to a colleague. Courtesy: Ramesh Sharma.

1986, *New Delhi Times*. 'The film is a Watergate-like movie about investigative journalism':
Shashi Kapoor. Courtesy: Ramesh Sharma.

1986, *New Delhi Times*. In this scene, Sharmila Tagore, playing a journalist's lawyer-wife,
consoles her husband, essayed by Shashi Kapoor, as the investigation gets
increasingly stressful. Courtesy: Ramesh Sharma.

it by someone who took offence to a dialogue where Vikas/Shashi
tells Nisha/Sharmila that all lawyers are liars; someone else tried
to get the film banned for depicting a politician instigating
communal riots. When *New Delhi Times* was scheduled to play on
Doordarshan, it was pulled out at the last minute because of the
legal battles that confronted it. To make matters worse, the film
was heavily pirated; after the first week, it became difficult to fill
large single-screen theatres. Ramesh rues: 'If we had multiplexes
then, as we do today, *New Delhi Times* would have played much
longer.'

New Delhi Times had already gone over-budget because of two
postponements—instead of the original Rs 25 lakh, it eventually
cost Rs 35 lakh. Now, assailed by a spate of lawsuits and piracy
concerns, the film gasped for survival. Ramesh, who kept in touch
with Shashi, recollects that the actor would occasionally ask him:
'*Kuch aa raha hai 5 per cent?*' ('Is the 5 per cent coming my way?')
Alas, there was no money to share.

Over the years, *New Delhi Times* has gone on to receive largely
positive reviews; critic Khalid Mohamed says: 'Only a scant few
films have achieved a semblance of truth-telling while discussing
the Fourth Estate. Of them, Ramesh Sharma's *New Delhi Times*, a
probe into the nexus between politicians and media barons, has
been the most incisive yet.'[5]

In 1986, *New Delhi Times* won the Indira Gandhi Award for
the best first film of a director, and Shashi's performance, which
was widely appreciated, garnered him a National Award for best
actor—the only time he won this honour. But for Shashi, it was
too little, too late. He went on to tell journalist Jyothi Venkatesh:

> I only wish they had given [the award] to my wife Jennifer
> when she was alive for her performance in my film *36
> Chowringhee Lane*. Frankly, the awards mean nothing to
> me at this stage when I do not have her to share it with
> me.[6]

Sammy and Rosie Get Laid (1987) and *The Deceivers* (1988)

In the mid-1980s, British filmmaker, Stephen Frears—today known for *High Fidelity*,[7] *Dirty Pretty Things*[8] and *The Queen*[9]— found himself on a flight to India at Ismail Merchant's behest.

Both Stephen and Ismail were at the cusp of new things. Stephen had just directed the explosive British–Asian film, *My Beautiful Laundrette*,[10] written by Hanif Kureishi, which explores the many facets (and especially the underbelly) of the Pakistani community in London, while detailing a gay romance between a young Pakistani man and his white schoolmate (seductively played by a young Daniel Day-Lewis). With the success of the film (Hanif's screenplay was nominated for an Oscar), Stephen was 'hot' in film festivals and art-house circles.

Ismail, in the meantime, had read John Masters' novel, *The Deceivers*[11]—a book detailing the 'thuggee' cult movement in British India through the story of William Savage, an East India Company official who infiltrates these marauding-murdering gangs, only to experience for himself the cult's immoderate bloodlust—and wished to make a film on it. Yet, neither James Ivory nor Ruth Prawer Jhabvala was excited about the idea, and Ismail was compelled to look beyond his comfort zone. On noticing Stephen's soaring popularity, he chose to grab not just this young director at his peak, but also a brand-new scriptwriter, playwright Charles Wood. (The project's core team would change along the way, and eventually, Michael Hirst, best known for the screenplay of *Elizabeth*,[12] would be the scriptwriter.)

This is how Stephen came to reach a bustling India. The moment he landed, one of the first things Ismail did was take him to meet Shashi Kapoor in his apartment in South Bombay. 'I was familiar with Shashi because I had seen *Shakespeare Wallah*,'[13] Stephen says. 'So, I knew he was very, very talented. But it was on meeting him that I realized that he was also a very sophisticated man.'

Stephen eventually decided not to pursue the film. 'We were quite devastated,' James says, when he learnt of the director's decision. Ismail writes in his autobiography that Stephen was not happy with the way the script of *The Deceivers* read.[14] But one observer, who shared a train with Stephen and Ismail while they were location-scouting, believes that India did not agree with the British director. Whatever may be the reason, *The Deceivers*[15] was eventually directed by Nicholas Meyer—best known for *Star Trek II: The Wrath of Khan*[16]—and Shashi played a supporting role in it, as an Indian landlord who would befriend the hero, William Savage (Pierce Brosnan). The film opened to mixed reviews, with some claiming that it 'cast quite a spell',[17] and others asserting that it was 'an adventure epic with a pretty measly sense of adventure.'[18]

What the film did do was earn Shashi another admirer; Pierce Brosnan would go on to praise Shashi's English, which was 'as good as any leading actor in Hollywood', and his 'effortless' performance. Then, he added: 'In one of the scenes, [Shashi] simply looked at me and smiled conveying a thousand words, which only an actor of high calibre can do.'[19]

*

Even while *The Deceivers* was being made, Stephen Frears and Shashi Kapoor found their paths crossing again; this time, the two actually did work together. What emerged was the second Hanif Kureishi-scripted film, *Sammy and Rosie Get Laid*.[20]

Sammy and Rosie Get Laid revolves around an unconventional, bohemian couple, with chaotic, yet hugely liberated, lives—until Rafi Rahman, Sammy's father, comes 'home' to England to revive his relationship with his son, daughter-in-law and a long-lost beloved. Even while attempting to renew ties, Rafi, we learn, is a man on the run from his corrupt and brutal past as a politician in Pakistan.

While Sammy, Rosie and Rafi play key roles in the film, a

fourth, equally significant character is the city of London. The British capital that Hanif conceived was taken from the pages of the newspapers of that time. Even as artists, activists, hippies and freethinkers partied hard, race riots and class wars rent the city during the peak of Margaret Thatcher's rule. The film brilliantly captures scenes of urban decline—gangs walk the streets that Rafi had once romanticized, and taxi drivers wear bloodied headbands. In more ways than one, the film is an angry letter to the British prime minister, and under Hanif's care, *Sammy and Rosie Get Laid* is charged with anarchic energy, coloured with the sexual politics of the era, and packed with questions of class and immigration.

Rafi's arrival in a collapsing city draws from Hanif's own observations. 'Sections are based on the experiences of one of my

1987, *Sammy and Rosie Get Laid*. Shashi Kapoor as Rafi with Claire Bloom, playing Alice. Rafi travels to London to rekindle his romance with her.

uncles who had come to London after a gap of thirty years—at a time of anti-Thatcher riots and uprisings in Brixton and St Pauls. London was on fire,' Hanif tells me. 'My uncle obviously had a very high opinion of the English, the BBC and how civilized this nation was. But now, he found this place a battlefield, with clashes between the police and the black kids.'

Besides his uncle, Hanif acknowledges that Rafi could also have been based on Zulfikar Ali Bhutto. 'I haven't met Bhutto, so I don't know him. But he was acquainted with my family—a very old friend of my father, someone he studied with in school,' he says. 'Like most of my older Indian or Pakistani characters, Rafi wasn't based on anyone specifically but was a mélange of various uncles and my thoughts on what it might have been like for a politician.'

To portray the complex role of Rafi, Hanif says he 'needed a very civilized, smooth, intelligent actor', someone who could play a Pakistani politician who'd enter a mad theatre of conflict and get 'surprised by the politics, the sexuality and the outrageousness'. For Hanif, Shashi was the ideal candidate.

Interestingly, Stephen reached the same conclusion. The director says, 'Back then, there weren't a lot of Indian actors who spoke English and had experience working in England. It really was quite a narrow choice. Then, to suddenly find this great Indian actor who was sophisticated—that was a real piece of luck, I thought. When I read Hanif's script, I knew this would be a role for Shashi.'

Yet, once they reached this joint casting decision, Hanif and Stephen were quite nervous that Shashi would not accept the part; after all, he was a star and the charisma he exuded was intimidating. Hanif writes in a diary he kept during the making of the film that the two met the Indian actor for lunch on 9 August 1986 at Notting Hill's '192', a restaurant that was amongst the biggest celebrity-magnets of the time. Shashi wore what Hanif describes as 'a loose brown costume, with a dark red and chocolate scarf flung over his shoulder […] He is so regal and dignified, stylish and exotic, that a shiver goes through the restaurant.'[21]

Despite the duo's apprehensions, Shashi—who Hanif describes as 'modest'—told the writer and director that he thought the script for *Sammy and Rosie Get Laid* was better than that of *My Beautiful Laundrette*; then, he added that he would be available to play the role of Rafi at the convenience of the filmmakers.

While one can understand Hanif and Stephen's eagerness to cast Shashi, one wonders: what made the actor accept a film with the team that made *My Beautiful Laundrette*—especially since, until then, at least internationally, he had only shown interest in the Merchant–Ivory team (with an occasional *Siddhartha*[22] and *Pretty Polly*[23])? Hanif speculates: 'Maybe Shashi thought, these kids—as we were then—are on to something exciting! So why don't I join them, have a go and see what they are doing?'

Hanif then goes on to acknowledge Jennifer Kendal Kapoor's influence, and Shashi's own desire to experiment, if only in a small British indie film. He says, 'If not this, Shashi would have played the same part over and over again in Hindi cinema. And he couldn't do that. He was a highly intelligent man. I have met many movie stars and most of them are really dull. Shashi, on the other hand, was well-read; he knew about cricket and all kinds of stuff. He didn't have a "Hollywood/Bollywood" kind of vacuity to him. He was a movie star, but he didn't want to look or sound like one.'

So it was—Ayub Khan-Din (who would later shine as the writer of the play and film, *East is East*[24]) was cast as Sammy; Frances Barber played Rosie; and a moustachioed, very elegant (though now overweight) forty-eight-year-old Shashi starred as the elderly Pakistani gentleman, Rafi. It was Shashi's own decision that Rafi don a moustache, and Hanif wholly approved. 'It makes him look older, less handsome, less of a matinee idol,' he writes in his diary. 'But [it also makes him] formidable, imposing and sort of British in the right military authoritarian sort of way.'[25]

As appreciative as he was of that moustache, Hanif (as also

Stephen) grew increasingly concerned about the actor's weight. Shashi agreed to slim down for the role; Stephen and Hanif even hoped to send the actor to a 'health farm', so he could 'look fitter and trimmer'. But apparently, the plan fell through when Shashi made it only just in time for the shoot. Hanif says, 'I remember discussing this issue with him. Shashi asked me, "Hanif, how can I get thin?" I said, "You have to eat less and exercise more." Then, Shashi responded, "I'm prepared to do anything but eat less and exercise more."' And that was where matters ended.

Shashi's weight proved to be a minor concern in comparison to what was to follow. On the first day of the shoot, when Hanif picked Shashi from his hotel, the actor seemed uncertain about the film's plot, even though he had read the script earlier. As mainstream Indian film stars often do, Shashi asked to be reminded of the story. It was this question that sent alarm bells ringing for Hanif. The scriptwriter wondered if Stephen and he had made the right casting choice. These doubts only increased when Shashi asked Stephen if he could leave early on the first day of the shoot since he had an invitation for a cocktail party. 'Frears said, if this is how stars behave, it might be difficult to deal with [him],' Hanif writes, sounding a bit worried himself in the diary.[26] 'But he's serious and keen,'[27] he later adds, as though trying desperately to reassure himself.

Fortunately, the early misgivings of the writer and director gave way to full-throated praise, as they watched Shashi at work. 'He participated absolutely enthusiastically,' Hanif says. 'He never thought for a moment that he was too good to work with rough kids like us. Really, everybody loved and adored him. He would go around, shake hands, say "good morning" to the crew—a perfect gentleman. He behaved without any vanity at all.' When recognized by London's South Asian population during shoots, Shashi displayed a similar kind of bonhomie—he'd greet his fans, even as they'd bring him food and take pictures.

Shashi also proved to be an actor who took things in his stride, no matter how demanding a shoot was. One of the final scenes in *Sammy and Rosie Get Laid* portrays a group of real estate developers clearing an area occupied by squatters. Among these unlawful residents is Rafi, spending the night in a trailer home, only to find it being bulldozed. In the film, Rafi is shown bouncing in a bed even as books tumble over his head. Clearly, this must have been a challenging scene for an actor used to certain creature comforts in the Hindi movie industry. Hanif seems to agree, as he writes in jest:

> When [Shashi] emerges, shaken and stirred, dizzy and fed up, he threatens to go back to Bombay. The next morning we tell him, as a joke, that we have to reshoot his scene in the back of the caravan, [and] he goes white.[28]

This is only one of several rare moments in *Sammy and Rosie Get Laid*, and Stephen's direction and Hanif's writing—which in Stephen's words, is always 'ironic about the English attitude towards Asians'—complement each other beautifully. In one hilarious scene, during a party at Sammy and Rosie's place, a guest, Anna (Wendy Gazelle), asks Rafi, 'Do you chant?' The scene reminds me of *The Householder*,[29] where an American woman asks Shashi's Prem Sagar about the kind of yoga he practises. Unlike Prem, who appears terribly confused by the question, Shashi's Rafi, who is over twenty years older, responds with breezy confidence: 'Chant what, my dear?' 'Mantras to keep yourself calm,' Anna says. To this, Rafi responds: 'I am calm. You young, international people mystify me. For you, the world and culture is like a departmental store. You come and take what you like from every floor. You have no attachments. For you, life is incoherent and shallow.' It is a terrific scene that needs to be watched to be fully appreciated—for Shashi is in his best form, with a wicked smile on his face, as he debunks Anna's clichéd understanding of Eastern philosophy.

Another clever scene unravels towards the middle of the film, when Stephen splits the screen into three horizontal segments to show six characters engaged in lovemaking—an overweight yet dashing Rafi in bed with Alice (Claire Bloom), his paramour from decades ago; Rosie, Rafi's daughter-in-law, having sex with Danny (the handsome Ronald Gift, also the lead singer of the music group, Fine Young Cannibals), and Sammy making out with Anna—all of this unspooling against The Ghetto Lites' reggae remix of Otis Redding's classic song, 'My Girl'.[30] Hanif writes: 'It is unashamedly erotic, a turn-on, running right up against the mean monogamous spirit of our age. There must be more jiggling of tongues in this film than in any other ever made.'[31]

When I saw *Sammy and Rosie Get Laid* with a group of friends in Boston, some of them were turned off by the film's sexual politics. I must admit, I was delighted when I witnessed their

1987, *Sammy and Rosie Get Laid*. Shashi Kapoor's Rafi looking shocked and confused at a party. By his side, Roland Gift, who plays Danny, is kissing Rafi's daughter-in-law, Rosie (Frances Barber).

discomfort. The film was special for me for another reason: it was in *Sammy and Rosie Get Laid* that I heard Nusrat Fateh Ali Khan's qawwalis for the first time.

Sammy and Rosie Get Laid opened in the US in late October 1987, and the critics were not very kind. Vincent Canby of *The New York Times* says: 'There's too much going on in Mr Kureishi's screenplay for any one person or thing to be satisfactorily explored [...] As each character is overwhelmed to a greater or lesser degree by contradictory impulses, so is the film.'[32] Pauline Kael of *The New Yorker* is equally harsh. 'There's no emotional force driving this movie,' she writes. 'There isn't even much wit in the film's cleverness.' But then, she adds: 'It's there in Kapoor's performance [...] Shashi Kapoor is marvelous as a man who adapts to whatever happens (or adapts up to a point).'[33]

The applause is well-deserved, for it's a role Shashi immersed himself in. When interviewed by *The New York Times*' Lawrence Van Gelder, Shashi says that while conventional wisdom holds that acting comes with nine 'rasas' or emotions,[34] Rafi's character demanded eighteen. 'I had to be good, I had to be bad, I had to be evil, I had to be funny, sometimes comical, and yet I had to be emotional—a very warm father, a warm, affectionate lover and yet [a] cunning, deceiving, selfish and a very fascist politician who had done probably horrendous things to achieve his goals. His character reminded me of Lear [...] I was fascinated by the part.'[35]

Lawrence goes on to suggest that Shashi is 'an Indian counterpart of Robert Redford or Steve McQueen'.[36] But the truth also is that at this stage in his career, Shashi was entirely in a league of his own.

In Custody (1993)

After the huge success of literary adaptations such as *A Room with a View*,[37] *Howards End*[38] and *The Remains of the Day*[39]—which cumulatively earned the Merchant–Ivory team six Oscars, apart

from box office credibility in Hollywood—Ismail Merchant chose
to return to his Indian roots. This time, he decided that he himself
would direct a film—*In Custody*[40]—his first feature, based on
author Anita Desai's novel by the same name.

In the book, shortlisted for the Man Booker Prize in 1984,
Anita narrates the heartbreaking tale of an old Urdu poet, Nur,
living his last days lost in a haze of alcohol, surrounded by his two
bickering wives—each occupying different floors of a dilapidated
haveli—and a group of young men, sycophants and chamchas in
wait of free booze and food. His only solace is the brief and sudden
arrival of a hapless teacher assigned to interview him for a literary
publication. In telling this story, *In Custody* enquires into the slow
death of a language. As Anita writes, through one of her characters:

> How will [Urdu] survive in this era of—the vegetarian
> monster, Hindi? [...] That language of peasants...the
> language that is raised on radishes and potatoes...yet like
> these vegetables, it flourishes, while Urdu—the language
> of the court in days of royalty—now languishes in the
> back lanes and gutters of the city. No place for it to live in
> the style to which it is accustomed, no emperors and
> nawabs to act as its patrons.[41]

Elsewhere, Anita (through Nur) asserts:

> How can there be Urdu poetry when there is no Urdu
> language left? It is dead, finished. The defeat of the
> Moghuls by the British threw a noose over its head, and
> the defeat of the British by the Hindi-wallahs tightened
> it. So now you see its corpse lying here, waiting to be
> buried.[42]

It is such commentary that captivated Ismail. In a 1999 event at
New York City's Asia Society, the director claimed that he was
attracted to the book's focus on Urdu poetry and the atmosphere

of a decaying culture. In his autobiography, Ismail further explains why he was drawn to the story of Urdu's collapse in modern India. 'Urdu is my language and my culture,' he writes. 'I saw this film as a homage to my heritage.'[43]

In Custody has a rich star cast. Om Puri plays the college teacher, Deven, wrenched at once by his love for Urdu that will grant him no monetary relief and the competing demands of a family which needs a source of income for sustenance—a duty he struggles to fulfil. While Shabana Azmi and Sushma Seth act as Nur's wives, Neena Gupta is Deven's disenchanted spouse.

1993, *In Custody*. An overweight Shashi Kapoor playing a melancholic poet, Nur. In this scene, Om Puri, as a college professor, is sent to interview Nur.
Courtesy: Merchant-Ivory Productions.

But first, there was the question of who'd play the overweight, tragic Nur. For Ismail, Shashi Kapoor was the immediate choice. However, this time, getting the actor on board wasn't easy, with Shashi being rather reluctant to accept the lead role. 'I kept on saying, I can't do it,' Shashi states in an interview. 'I don't know the language, I have never been to the Urdu poets' mushairas. I had known some [...] like Kaifi Azmi—a very renowned Urdu poet who was my father's neighbour. But I have never studied [the] life of a poet. And I was very scared to speak pure, good Urdu and pure Farsi.'[44]

A hesitant Shashi went on to recommend to Ismail the names of other actors who were, in his view, more worthy of the role, including Dilip Kumar. But Ismail remained unconvinced, and finally, after a few years, the director—well-known for his persistence—managed to convince those close to Shashi (his children and his brother, Shammi Kapoor) that this would be a dream project for the actor. After that, 'taming' Shashi was easy. The actor admits as much—that after Ismail made 'everyone to kind of side with him [he managed to] brainwash me into accepting the part and doing it.'[45]

Perhaps the biggest testimony to Ismail's persuasive powers is that he got the novel's author to write the film's script (which was translated into Urdu by Shahrukh Husain). He also used the poems of Faiz Ahmed Faiz, written well before the film was conceived; today, they seem so organic to the plot that it's though they were commissioned for the film. At the Asia Society event, Ismail says that the use of Faiz's work seemed obvious to him since Anita had, in fact, kept the Pakistani poet at the back of her mind while writing *In Custody*. It's quite a coincidence, then, that Faiz died in 1984, the same year that Anita's novel was published.

Although the novel is set in Delhi, Ismail shifted the location to Bhopal, a city he refers to as a centre of art and culture in India. While James Ivory was not involved with the production of the film, he flew down to Bhopal to watch the shoot for a couple of weeks; he'd visit the sets every day during this period and observe Shashi at work. One morning, out of the blue, Ismail told him that he was tired. "'I want to take a nap,'" he said to me. "'You direct the next scene,'" James reveals. 'It was a shot with Shashi and Om, and the kid (Chiku played by Sagar Arya) was supposed to tape-record the interviews. Shashi was in bed and kept lapsing into English poetry. While the kid remained unsure about whether he ought to turn on the mic, Om kept pushing him. I directed that scene and it was a lot of fun working with Shashi again, to be back on set with him.' For Shashi, too, it must have been a special day—to be directed by the man who had given him one of his first breaks in *The Householder* and who had secured for him early international acclaim.

James thinks that *In Custody* is among Shashi's finest performances. He says, 'Recently, many of our Indian films were shown in Honolulu and I watched *In Custody* all the way through. It's a terrific film—very moving and unusual. And Shashi was great.' Shashi, too, was satisfied with his portrayal of Nur. 'I am pleased, so happy [I acted as the poet],' Shashi says. 'I am very proud of the fact that I could play somebody very alien to me, very different from me, *very* unknown to me.'[46]

In Custody received strong reviews in the US, and Caryn James of *The New York Times* was full of praise for Shashi:

> Nur is a curiously imposing figure, even with his back to the camera, and provides what may be the greatest role in the long career of Shashi Kapoor. [...] Almost thirty years ago, Mr. Kapoor was the slender, handsome youth in the early Merchant–Ivory film *Shakespeare Wallah*, and more recently the outraged father in Stephen Frears' *Sammy and Rosie Get Laid*. In Ismail Merchant's rich and enticing *In Custody*, Mr. Kapoor turns Nur into a present-day Balzac: fierce and wise, yet with all the signs of having lived a little too well.[47]

While Caryn says that Ismail crams his first directorial venture with all his affection for Indian culture—making the film at times

seem like it is serving 'the stately function of artistic ambassador'—
she adds that the film is buoyed by its actors: '*In Custody* never
loses sight of the confused humanity of its heroes, so strongly
played by Mr. Kapoor and Mr. Puri.'[48]

The calibre of the actors, and especially Shashi (in a corpulent
avatar), comes to be commented upon in other film reviews.
Variety's Derek Elley writes: 'As the burnt-out, roly-poly bard,
[Shashi] Kapoor, almost unrecognizable from his slim, matinee-
idol days, limns a commanding presence, halfway between an
Indian [Charles] Laughton and [Sydney] Greenstreet.'[49] And
Washington Post's Rita Kempley writes, '[Shashi] Kapoor, a
bellowing buffalo of an actor, recalls Orson Welles as he lies about
in a gouty heap, bemoaning his artistic atrophy to a band of
drunken groupies.'[50]

While Shashi's weight was often brought up as way of praising
his performance (with simultaneous references to other Western
actors who were also portly), and while his pudginess may have
helped him sink into the character of Nur, Shabana remembers
some difficult moments during the shoot precisely on account of
the actor's heft. She says, 'Shashi had put on huge amounts of
weight and it was painful to see him lying flat on the ground after
an alcoholic fit. I used to feel very bad.' Sanjna Kapoor adds, 'Papa
used to drink quite a lot at that time. He got into the habit of
drinking a bottle of vodka a day.'

Then, as the person who knows Shashi best and also as his
harshest critic, Sanjna adds, 'I think Papa wasn't as fantastic as he
should have been in *In Custody*. He prettied up things a bit too
much for the role—*he* was too pretty. I would have liked to see a
little more decay. The film left me wanting more.'

In Custody ends with the funeral procession of Nur. The poet's
coffin is carried out of his dilapidated haveli into the streets, even
as his widows, surrounded by their servants, watch on from the
two levels of their residence. Crowds gather around the coffin,
with some people even carrying it. In the background we hear

Hariharan's rendition of Faiz's poem, 'Aaj Bazaar Mein Pa-ba Joulaan Chalo', roughly translated as 'Today We Must Walk the Market Place in Shackles'.[51]

Recalling that scene, James tells me, 'The moment was re-enacted. I was not in Bombay after Ismail died—while he passed away in London, his funeral was in Bombay. I later learned that Shashi had led all the mourners through the streets of the city. I thought, what a strange—no, more than strange—how odd, the symmetry of something like that. How poignant, the emotional depth.' James' description stays with me as a rare instance of life imitating art.

Jinnah (1998)

For the fiftieth anniversary of the creation of Pakistan, filmmaker Jamil Dehlavi and co-writer/executive producer Akbar Ahmed set out to make a definitive film on the founding father of their country—Muhammad Ali Jinnah—a film that some would refer to as Pakistan's response to Richard Attenborough's *Gandhi*.[52] But the project got delayed by a year and *Jinnah*[53] was finally completed in 1998.

The aim of *Jinnah*, Jamil says, was three-fold: to correct history; to present the liberal side of Islam; and to bring to life a person largely unknown to younger Pakistanis both at home and abroad.[54] But to achieve this objective, Jamil was not interested in making a linear biopic. Instead, his script went back and forth in time, while tracing the different facets of Jinnah's life. In a rare departure from convention, the flashbacks unspool as the dead leader's soul takes a long walk with an angel—who, in turn, examines Jinnah's life, balancing his good deeds against the contentious ones and arriving at a final judgement. Akbar is quoted as saying, 'It was Jamil's idea to move the straightforward script into the realm of fantasy. He felt it would be more exciting this way. Initially I was uncomfortable, but I realized it would make for a better film.'[55]

1998, *Jinnah*. Shashi Kapoor, as the 'narrator', weighs the sins of Muhammad Ali Jinnah (Christopher Lee). Courtesy: Jamil Dehlavi.

1998, *Jinnah*. Shashi Kapoor remains quizzical as the 'narrator' judging Muhammad Ali Jinnah's life. Courtesy: Jamil Dehlavi.

1998, *Jinnah*. Shashi Kapoor, the 'narrator', with a book on Jinnah's life.
Courtesy: Jamil Dehlavi.

1998, *Jinnah*. Shashi Kapoor, the 'narrator', watches on as Muhammad Ali Jinnah
revisits key moments of his life. Courtesy: Jamil Dehlavi.

Jamil wished to sign on an international cast, particularly because he could not get a Pakistani star to play Jinnah in an English language film. 'Most of the Pakistani actors I have worked with— well, they are not comfortable acting in English,' Jamil tells me. 'Their performances end up being quite stilted. So, I faced the huge challenge of finding an actor who looked like Jinnah and could carry off the role and the myth—which is why I signed on Christopher Lee, who is terrific.'

For the part of the angel, Jamil decided to cast Shashi Kapoor. 'We needed somebody who was a strong actor, a star equal to Christopher, and also a little quirky, with a slightly humorous dimension to him. Shashi seemed like an obvious choice. He wasn't the young superstar he used to be and I thought he could pull off the idiosyncrasies of the character.' Jamil also believed that Shashi's weight-gain interacted rather well with the character of the enquiring angel that he was playing.

However, in the final cut of *Jinnah*, I point out, the angel is called the narrator; Jamil tells me why there was a change in script: 'When you make films in this part of the world, you have to be very careful, because you can hurt people's sensitivities. You can cause a controversy for no reason.' Shashi must have been alerted to the dangers of playing 'Archangel Gabriel', because later, when he was asked in an interview about his character in *Jinnah*, he quickly said, 'Oh no! I'm not playing the archangel. There is [no such character] in the film. I play the role of the narrator—it is similar to the role of the sutradhar in Indian [drama]; it's like the chorus in the plays of Shakespeare.' Then he added, 'My character is in limbo; it's a mix of fiction and [all things] abstract.'[56]

Despite Shashi and Jamil's cautiousness, *Jinnah* ran into serious trouble. To begin with, malicious rumours began appearing in local newspapers. During the eleven-week shoot in Karachi, the casting of Christopher stirred heated protests. In September 1998, a BBC report quoted arts correspondent, Razia Iqbal, as saying, 'It is the fact that Mr. Lee is associated with Count Dracula and not that he is a European playing an Asian that has exercised people.'[57] Activists reportedly demanded Christopher's arrest and deportation from Pakistan. Those were tense times, and the producers found themselves providing armed guards for the British actor. In addition, they had to offer security cover to Shashi. 'Not that there is any problem,' Shashi tries clarifying in an interview. 'I do move about, I go to people's houses for lunches, to the Sindh Club. It's a very nice place, with really great people. [...] The atmosphere is very congenial.' Ever reasonable, Shashi adds, '*Apne hi log hain, yaar.* (They are our own kind.) The same people, the same culture, you don't feel like you are shooting outside India.'[58]

Then came news of the Pakistani government—one of the original backers of *Jinnah*—withdrawing funding halfway through the film. Jamil had to make some quick revisions—among them, chopping Shashi's role to some extent. 'There was a segment where Shashi and Jinnah transcend time, meet modern Muslim leaders, people like Saddam Hussein,' Jamil explains. 'It was quite an interesting strand in the film. But we couldn't finish it. We had run out of money.'

Regardless of these complications, Shashi has poignant memories of the shoot—one of them involving Christopher in the middle of a huge gathering of onlookers. 'The crowd scenes are very moving to watch,' he says as part of a film interview. 'When Jinnah walks through the crowds, we actually had old men who were not part of the crew touching him... It reminded me of... the shooting of *Gandhi*...in Bombay and Delhi. The people here treat him with such reverence.'[59]

As for Jamil, he fondly remembers the time he spent with Shashi: 'Shashi is such a wonderful man, very unassuming. Actually, I was pleasantly surprised, because he has a huge track record and he could well have been difficult. But no, not at all, he wasn't. He was humble, easy to work with.' In *Jinnah*, a stout Shashi, dressed in a starched white kurta-pyjama, walks with a beatific smile on his face, almost as though he's enjoying every minute of being the 'narrator'.

It is a role where Shashi proves to be the perfect foil to Christopher. While Shashi says he loved working with the British star ('He is a marvellous actor,' he asserts, 'besides being a good human being, very conscious of the responsibility that he carries playing the role of the Quaid-e-Azam'[60]), Christopher, too, remained gracious during a 2001 radio interview with the Pakistan News Service: 'The Pakistani actors in the film were very kind to me and we had a very distinguished Indian actor in the film, Shashi Kapoor.'[61]

In December 1998, *Jinnah* received a strong positive review in the *Los Angeles Times*, with the critic, Kevin Thomas, praising the actors: 'By the time the film is over, Lee is tremendously moving in his ability to illuminate the inner life of a man of unflinching dignity [...] The cast is outstanding, including the witty Kapoor (long a mainstay of Indian cinema).'[62] It is a review that encapsulates the merits of *Jinnah*—a film that captures the essence of a man who may have been exceedingly correct, reserved, even dour—but who, despite these constraints in disposition, emerges as a leader of enormous courage and uncompromising rectitude.

If the movie falters, it is on account of the fact that, in a bid to offer a rejoinder to *Gandhi*, which depicts Jinnah as a power-hungry man, Jamil's film—in the words of a critic—'ends up presenting a Manichean world in which Jinnah stands for the "good" while Gandhi, Nehru, and Mountbatten together form an "evil" triumvirate over which Jinnah prevails [... lowering an] otherwise commendable effort to the level of [...] hero-worship.'[63] Professor Paul Vallely points out that the film, rather ironically, managed to 'achieve the unenviable distinction of being attacked in India as Pakistani propaganda and in Jinnah's home country as both a Hindu and a Zionist plot.'[64]

Jinnah did not make it to the movie theatres, and was released as a DVD seven years after it was made, in 2005, for want of a distributor. For Christopher, who otherwise had an illustrious track record, it remained a huge regret. 'It had the best reviews I've ever had in my entire career—as a film and as a performance,' he says in a BBC report,[65] expressing his bewilderment at *Jinnah*'s inability to achieve the success it deserved.

Side Streets (1998)

In the late 1990s, Tony Gerber, a young New York-based documentary filmmaker, set out to make his first feature film that he co-wrote with his wife, Lynn Nottage. *Side Streets*[66] is a slice of New York life, with a series of intersecting immigrant tales, each set in one of the five boroughs of New York City on a particularly hot summer day.

Among the stories scripted was that of an Indian–American limousine driver, Bipin Raj, living on Staten Island with his wife Chandra, their kids, and a new addition to his family—his brother, Vikram Raj. Fleeing from the reality that his career as a big Hindi movie actor is over, Vikram—no doubt enigmatic at one point, but now an overweight alcoholic with delusions of grandeur—becomes an altogether demanding guest, much to Chandra's dismay.

To depict the rather complex role of an increasingly frustrated Chandra—who has to kowtow to Vikram's demands for more air-conditioning or a better breakfast, while he lounges around, basking in the adulation he had once known, or in the belief that Al Pacino will call—Tony and Lynn considered casting Shabana Azmi. In September 1996, when one of the producers met the actress at the Toronto International Film Festival—where she was promoting Deepa Mehta's *Fire*[67]—Shabana agreed to play the part. While Art Malik would join the film as Shabana's limousine driver husband, the actress suggested to the filmmakers that Shashi Kapoor could quite easily play the role of the ageing former actor,

Vikram. When she returned to Bombay, Shabana promptly passed
the script to Shashi. 'He was very interested although he contacted
me saying that he didn't have an agent in the US,' Tony tells me.
'But he added that effectively Ismail Merchant was his agent.' So,
Ismail came on board, acting as an intermediary for Shashi, and
along the way, becoming the executive producer, too.

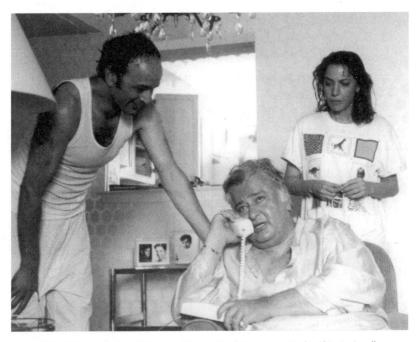

1998, *Side Streets*. Shashi Kapoor as Vikram, the fading star, waits for Al Pacino's call.
Shabana Azmi (background) watches as the harried wife of a limousine driver,
played by Art Malik (left). Photo credit: Seth Rubin. Courtesy: Side Streets Productions.

Side Streets inadvertently became the third part of an unofficial
trilogy for Shashi—with *Sammy and Rosie Get Laid* and *In Custody*
being the first two parts. In each of the films, the actor plays the
role of an ageing, overweight man, a mere shadow of the giant he
had been at the height of his career—he's a politician escaping a
past in *Sammy and Rosie Get Laid*, a poet lamenting the passage

of time in *In Custody*, and an actor left with only memories of past glory in *Side Streets*.

Like so many others I speak to, Tony tells me that Shashi was a thorough professional. 'He was a wonderful actor,' the director says. 'The thing I specifically remember about him is that, unlike other stars—who finish their lines and then drop character, or look to the director, asking, "We're done, right? We got it?"—Shashi would stay in a scene until I called "cut".'

So, Tony began playing a game with Shashi, where he started delaying his call. 'It was really fun,' he laughs, 'rolling the camera, while Shashi filled every moment. I had a non-verbal cue for the crew, so Shashi would not know when I called "cut" and he would do incredible things. He was a much better actor than I expected him to be!' Tony also remembers that Shashi was quick to grasp situations and perform. 'On an average,' he says, 'Shashi would give three takes and, by then, he would have nailed the part; he didn't need longer than that. Sometimes, he'd give a range of performances for each take. However, if I demanded a fourth take or a fifth, he'd inevitably start going downhill. I don't think it had to do with his energy or his physical condition. I believe it was because he would move on mentally and creatively.'

Yet, it is a fact that by the time he had committed to *Side Streets*, Shashi had ceased being entirely well; he had been emotionally wrenched by the loss of his wife, and was curtailed by a body that would not support him. Tony tells me that, through the shoot, there had been some concern about his ankles swelling.

Then, there was the night when the crew was about to shoot the last scene with the actor. But Shashi said he was tired. 'He did appear exhausted and cranky, and he decided he didn't want to perform,' Lynn and Tony say. But then, they faced their own set of production problems. 'The entire crew was there, we had already picked the hotel, and we didn't have the money to send the crew home. It was one of the more expensive shoot days,' they point out. 'But Shashi had locked the hotel door! We begged him to come out.' Shashi had only done a couple of takes for the day, so his overwhelming sense of fatigue was odd—but Tony explains that his weariness might have been more than just physical: 'You know, the scene concerned his death,' Tony says. 'Maybe he found himself going to a dark place. '

Eventually, Shashi managed to open the door to his room. He emerged, got dressed in a silk orange kurta-pyjama, and performed a bhangra-like dance to 'Le Jayenge, Le Jayenge, Dilwale Dulhania Le Jayenge'[68] from *Chor Machaye Shor*.[69] Lynn says, 'After we convinced him to do this marvellous dance, he surrendered everything to it and performed so wonderfully—and all in one take—that the crew spontaneously clapped at the end. It was a beautiful moment and you could see Shashi digging deep into his soul to conjure it—all along conscious that he was heavy and he was tired.'

Shashi ends the scene with a recitation of 'Abhi To Main Jawaan Hun'—the deeply ironic poem by Pakistani poet, Hafeez Jalandhari; the poet knows he is in a race against time, but rages against the onslaught of old age:

> *Ye kya gumaan hai badgumaan, samajh na mujh ko naatavaan*
> *Khayaal-e-zohd, abhi kahaan? Abhi to main jawaan hun.*
>
> *(Spare me your doubts, those apprehensions of decay.*
> *Abstinence—ah, isn't it too soon for that? For now, I am still*
> *young.)*

To date, I feel enormously sad watching Shashi deliver those lines. We know what he was like in his youth and we now see him, a completely transformed man. Yet the actor in him still burns strong, and it is on full display in *Side Streets*—his penultimate film, followed by *Dirty British Boys*[70] a year later.

Variety's critic, David Rooney, while offering a tepid review for *Side Streets* (calling it 'overlong' but 'likeable'), is unstinted in his praise for Shashi 'whose role here contains ironic echoes of his own career. He plays the has-been star as both arrogant and deflated, dignified and pathetic, gradually shifting from understated comedy to pathos in the most poignant of the stories' conclusions.'[71] It is this that especially strikes the viewer—the self-referentiality of the Staten Island segment of *Side Streets*. Vikram is Shashi, and their lives, marked by a rare kind of despair, mirror each other.

While Shashi was not a demanding actor, Tony followed Ismail's suggestion and provided him with two assistants—young Indians in New York City—Rohena Gera (today known as the script/story writer for *Kuch Naa Kaho*[72] and *Thoda Pyaar Thoda Magic*[73] and the director of the documentary, *What's Love Got to Do with It?*[74]) and Sabrina Dhawan (now known as the scriptwriter for *Monsoon Wedding*,[75] *Kaminey*[76] and *Ishqiya*[77]). Both have strong recollections of their time with Shashi.

1998, *Side Streets*. Shashi Kapoor with the film's executive producer, Ismail Merchant and director, Tony Gerber (l-r). Photo credit: Seth Rubin. Courtesy: Side Streets Productions.

Rohena remembers sitting outside the Staten Island house where the Shashi, Art and Shabana segments were shot, and especially recollects Shashi's warmth. The actor, she tells me, far from being dismissive, was curious about her—this young Indian graduate from Sarah Lawrence College, interested in films. Over a Chinese lunch in Manhattan, he tried helping her with her career by asking if she would consider working as part of the New York crew for his nephew, Rishi Kapoor's movie, *Aa Ab Laut Chalen*.[78] 'I subsequently met Chintu (Rishi),' Rohena says, 'but it wasn't a good fit for me. Throughout, Shashi Kapoor remained very sweet about it—dignified and generous, but not odd. Being a single woman in the film business, one is often wary, but he was like a warm, caring uncle.'

Curiously, this is the precise sketch Sabrina offers. She had come on board *Side Streets* as a cultural consultant for the film, finding songs from Shashi's classics, and recalls being especially excited about meeting the star. 'I hadn't met many actors,' she tells me, 'since I was a student at that time. So, it surprised me initially when I learnt that they are *real* people, too—or at least, Shashi Kapoor was. He could be your favourite uncle!'

Sabrina also found in Shashi a rare kind of humility. She says, a day after Shabana arrived for the shoot, she overheard Shashi and the actress conversing in a corner—'in Hindi, which is code language if you are a foreigner or an immigrant,' Sabrina says. 'Shabana Azmi whispered, "*Yahan kuch khane peene ko hai?*" ("Is there anything to eat or drink here?") and Shashi Kapoor unassumingly replied, "*Pata nahin, bahar kuch biscuit-viscuit, bagel-shagel pade hue hain.*" ("I don't know, but there's a biscuit or a bagel outside.") There was something really endearing about that moment, so sweet—to hear an iconic movie star say this almost guilelessly.'

Sabrina adds: 'Shashi Kapoor was incredibly refined and polite. It isn't the kind of civility that exists in Bombay today. His was inbred and sincere. The elegance, the sophistication was real. There was something movingly old world about him. It makes you wish that people like him could live forever.'

'Yes,' I can only whisper. 'Yes, it does.'

Notes

1. 1978, *Rumtek: A Monastery Wreathed in a Hundred Thousand Rainbows*, dir. Ramesh Sharma, prod. Ramesh Sharma.
2. 1986, *New Delhi Times*, dir. Ramesh Sharma, prod. P.K. Tiwari, starring Shashi Kapoor, Sharmila Tagore, Om Puri.
3. 1965, *Waqt*, dir. Yash Chopra, prod. B.R. Chopra, starring Balraj Sahni, Sharmila Tagore, Shashi Kapoor.
4. Lawrence Van Gelder, 'At the Movies', *The New York Times*, 13 November 1987.
5. Khalid Mohamed, 'The Fourth Estate: From Real and Reel', *Khaleej Times*, 13 December 2013.
6. Jyothi Venkatesh, 'Shashi Kapoor', *Frontline*, 14-27 June 1986.
7. 2000, *High Fidelity*, dir. Stephen Frears, prod. Tim Bevan, Rudd Simmons, starring John Cusack, Jack Black, Lisa Bonet.
8. 2002, *Dirty Pretty Things*, dir. Stephen Frears, prod. Tracey Seaward, Robert Jones, starring Chiwetel Ejiofor, Audrey Tautou, Sergi López.
9. 2006, *The Queen*, dir. Stephen Frears, prod. Andy Harries, Christine Langan, Tracey Seaward, starring Helen Mirren, Michael Sheen, James Cromwell.
10. 1985, *My Beautiful Laundrette*, dir. Stephen Frears, prod. Sarah Radclyffe, Tim Bevan, starring Gordon Warnecke, Daniel Day-Lewis, Saeed Jaffrey.
11. John Masters, *The Deceivers* (New York: Carroll & Graf, 1988).
12. 1998, *Elizabeth*, dir. Shekhar Kapur, prod. Tim Bevan, Eric Fellner, Alison Owen, starring Cate Blanchett, Geoffrey Rush, Joseph Fiennes.
13. 1965, *Shakespeare Wallah*, dir. James Ivory, prod. Ismail Merchant, starring Shashi Kapoor, Felicity Kendal, Madhur Jaffrey.
14. Ismail Merchant, *My Passage from India: A Filmmaker's Journey from Bombay to Hollywood* (New York: Viking Studio, 2002), p. 115.
15. 1988, *The Deceivers*, dir. Nicholas Meyer, prod. Ismail Merchant, starring Pierce Brosnan, Shashi Kapoor, Saeed Jaffrey.
16. 1982, *Star Trek II: The Wrath of Khan*, dir. Nicholas Meyer, prod. Robert Sallin, starring William Shatner, Leonard Nimoy, DeForest Kelley.

17. Jay Boyar, 'The Deceivers: Review', *Orlando Sentinel*, 17 February 1989.
18. Hal Hinson, 'The Deceivers' Missed Metaphor', *The Washington Post*, 9 September 1988.
19. Quoted in Pradip Gupta, 'James Bond Wishes Shashi Kapoor', *The Times of India*, 17 March 2011.
20. 1987, *Sammy and Rosie Get Laid*, dir. Stephen Frears, prod. Tim Bevan, Sarah Radclyffe, starring Shashi Kapoor, Frances Barber, Claire Bloom.
21. Hanif Kureishi, 'Some Time With Stephen', *London Kills Me: Three Screenplays And Four Essays* (New York: Penguin 1992), p. 124.
22. 1972, *Siddhartha*, dir. Conrad Rooks, prod. Conrad Rooks, starring Shashi Kapoor, Simi Garewal, Romesh Sharma.
23. 1967, *Pretty Polly*, dir. Guy Green, prod. George W. George, Frank Granat, starring Hayley Mills, Shashi Kapoor, Trevor Howard.
24. 1999, *East is East*, dir. Damien O'Donnell, prod. Leslee Udwin, starring Om Puri, Linda Bassett, Archie Panjabi.
25. Hanif Kureishi, 'Some Time With Stephen', *London Kills Me: Three Screenplays And Four Essays* (New York: Penguin 1992), pp. 155–56.
26. *Ibid.*, p. 151.
27. *Ibid.*, p. 155.
28. *Ibid.*, p. 162.
29. 1963, *The Householder*, dir. James Ivory, prod. Ismail Merchant, starring Shashi Kapoor, Leela Naidu, Durga Khote.
30. 'My Girl', lyr. Smokey Robinson, Ronald White, comp. William Robinson, Ronald White, artist Otis Redding.
31. Hanif Kureishi, 'Some Time With Stephen', *London Kills Me: Three Screenplays And Four Essays* (New York: Penguin 1992), p. 183.
32. Vincent Canby, 'Film: Sammy and Rosie', *The New York Times*, 30 October 1987.
33. Pauline Kael, 'The Current Cinema: Sammy and Rosie Get Laid,' *The New Yorker*, 16 November 1987.
34. The concept of 'navarasa' or 'nine emotions' is indebted to Bharata Muni's ancient work of dramatic theory, *Natyasastra*, written sometime between 200 BC and 200 AD. The nine 'rasas' include shringara (love), hasya (laughter), karuna (compassion), raudra (anger), veera (courage), bhayanaka (terror), bheebhatsya (disgust), adbutha (surprise) and shantha (peace). See Bharata Muni, *The Natyasastra: English Translation with Critical Notes*, translated by Adya Rangacharya (New Delhi: Munshiram, 2014).
35. Lawrence Van Gelder, 'At the Movies', *The New York Times*, 13 November 1987.

36. *Ibid.*
37. 1985, *A Room with a View*, dir. James Ivory, prod. Ismail Merchant, starring Maggie Smith, Helena Bonham Carter, Denholm Elliott.
38. 1992, *Howards End*, dir. James Ivory, prod. Ismail Merchant, starring Anthony Hopkins, Vanessa Redgrave, Helena Bonham Carter.
39. 1993, *The Remains of the Day*, dir. James Ivory, prod. Ismail Merchant, John Calley, Mike Nichols, starring John Haycraft, Christopher Reeve, Anthony Hopkins.
40. 1993, *In Custody*, dir. Ismail Merchant, prod. Wahid Chowhan, starring Shashi Kapoor, Shabana Azmi, Om Puri.
41. Anita Desai, *In Custody* (New Delhi: Random House, 2007), p. 14.
42. *Ibid.*, p. 45.
43. Ismail Merchant, *My Passage from India: A Filmmaker's Journey from Bombay to Hollywood* (New York: Viking Studio, 2002), p. 124.
44. Based on an interview with Shashi Kapoor in the Criterion Collection DVD of *In Custody*.
45. *Ibid.*
46. *Ibid.*
47. Caryn James, 'Review/Film: Ismail Merchant Directs First Feature', *The New York Times*, 15 April 1994.
48. *Ibid.*
49. Derek Elley, 'Review', *Variety*, 21 November 1993.
50. Rita Kempley, 'In Custody', *The Washington Post*, 30 April 1994.
51. 'Aaj Bazaar Mein Pa-ba Joulaan Chalo', lyr. Faiz Ahmed Faiz, comp. Ustad Zakir Hussain, artist Hariharan.
52. 1982, *Gandhi*, dir. Richard Attenborough, prod. Richard Attenborough, starring Ben Kingsley, Rohini Hattangadi, Roshan Seth.
53. 1998, *Jinnah*, dir. Jamil Dehlavi, prod. Jamil Dehlavi, starring Christopher Lee, Shashi Kapoor, Maria Aitken.
54. See 'Jinnah on the Silverscreen', *Columbia University*, in <http://www.columbia.edu/itc/mealac/pritchett/00litlinks/naim/txt_naim_onjinnah.pdf>, accessed on 11 January 2016.
55. Quoted in an interview with Fatima Yamin, *Dawn*, 18 April 1999.
56. Quoted in Suparn Verma, 'Christopher Lee Playing Jinnah is Like Mukri Playing Gandhi', *Rediff*, in <http://www.rediff.com/news/apr/05jinnah.htm>, accessed on 8 January 2015.
57. In 'Troubled Jinnah Movie Opens', *BBC*, 26 September 1998.
58. Quoted in Suparn Verma, 'Christopher Lee Playing Jinnah is Like Mukri Playing Gandhi', *Rediff*, in <http://www.rediff.com/news/apr/05jinnah.htm>, accessed on 8 January 2015.

59. *Ibid.*
60. *Ibid.*
61. Aisha Fayyazi Sarwari in an interview with Christopher Lee, 2001.
62. Kevin Thomas, 'Bringing Little-Known Pakistani Leader Jinnah to Life', *Los Angeles Times*, 15 December 1998.
63. 'Jinnah on the Silverscreen', *Columbia University*, in <http://www.columbia.edu/itc/mealac/pritchett/00litlinks/naim/txt_naim_onjinnah.pdf>, accessed on 11 January 2016.
64. Paul Vallely, 'Was Jinnah a Saint or Sinner?', *Independent*, 13 November 1998.
65. Quoted in 'Obituary: Christopher Lee', *BBC*, 11 June 2015.
66. 1998, *Side Streets*, dir. Tony Gerber, prod. Bruce Weiss, starring Valeria Golino, Shashi Kapoor, Shabana Azmi.
67. 1996, *Fire*, dir. Deepa Mehta, prod. Bobby Bedi, Deepa Mehta, starring Shabana Azmi, Nandita Das, Javed Jaffrey.
68. 'Le Jayenge, Le Jayenge, Dilwale Dulhania Le Jayenge', lyr. Inderjeet Singh Tulsi, comp. Ravindra Jain, artists Asha Bhosle, Kishore Kumar.
69. 1974, *Chor Machaye Shor*, dir. Ashok Roy, prod. N.N. Sippy, starring Shashi Kapoor, Mumtaz, Danny Denzongpa.
70. 1999, *Dirty British Boys*, dir. Assad Raja, prod. Fraz Hussain, starring George Cristopher, Shashi Kapoor, Assad Raja.
71. David Rooney, 'Review: "Side Streets"', *Variety*, 7 October 1998.
72. 2003, *Kuch Naa Kaho*, dir. Rohan Sippy, prod. Ramesh Sippy, starring Abhishek Bachchan, Aishwarya Rai, Satish Shah.
73. 2008, *Thoda Pyaar Thoda Magic*, dir. Kunal Kohli, prod. Aditya Chopra, Kunal Kohli, starring Rishi Kapoor, Saif Ali Khan, Rani Mukherjee.
74. *What's Love Got to Do with It?*, dir. Rohena Gera, prod. Rohena Gera.
75. 2001, *Monsoon Wedding*, dir. Mira Nair, prod. Caroline Baron, Mira Nair, starring Naseeruddin Shah, Lilette Dubey, Shefali Shah.
76. 2009, *Kaminey*, dir. Vishal Bhardwaj, prod. Ronnie Screwvala, starring Shahid Kapoor, Priyanka Chopra, Deb Mukherjee.
77. 2010, *Ishqiya*, dir. Abhishek Chaubey, prod. Raman Maroo, starring Naseeruddin Shah, Vidya Balan, Arshad Warsi.
78. 1999, *Aa Ab Laut Chalen*, dir. Rishi Kapoor, prod. Rajiv Kapoor, Rishi Kapoor, Randhir Kapoor, starring Rajesh Khanna, Akshaye Khanna, Aishwarya Rai.

7

THINGS FALL APART
Shashi after Jennifer

In Jennifer Kendal Kapoor's life, the domestic, at least for a while, superseded all else. Even as Shashi got increasingly busy with his career as an actor–producer, Jennifer abandoned her vocation as an actress to keep home and raise her three children.

Perhaps, 'abandoned' is a poor choice of word, since, in an interview, Jennifer says that there was never a point when she wasn't committed to the life of a theatre actor:

> I never quit theatre as such. Had I known then that I was going to be away from the stage for so long, I would've reacted very badly. I would've been very disturbed. I've still got my hand towel, in which we used to have liquid paraffin to wipe off our make-up. It's still in my make-up case. It's just as I left it after the last show I did. I've always had this superstition: I felt that if I washed it, I would never act again.[1]

It was Jennifer's love for theatre that propelled her to start Prithvi and look into its day-to-day management and functioning. And it was her love for acting that drew her back to cinema after a long

1970, *Bombay Talkie*. Shashi Kapoor in a passionate moment with the British writer, played by his wife, Jennifer Kendal Kapoor. Courtesy: Merchant-Ivory Productions.

break with *36 Chowringhee Lane*.[2] Following the critical acclaim the film received, Jennifer was suddenly in the limelight, her career as an actress resurrected. Offers began pouring in, and soon, she found herself playing Mrs Saunders—that cheerless woman in perpetual fear of being molested by an Indian servant—in *Heat and Dust*.[3] But now, when she had the time to act, her health refused to support her.

It was 1983. Cannes. Jennifer —who, until then, was thought to be suffering from amoebic dysentery—was diagnosed with cancer. Geoffrey Kendal writes in his autobiography that when he learnt of his daughter's malady, he could not utter the word 'cancer' for the longest time; he called it 'the illness' or 'this thing'.[4]

In the meantime, Jennifer, in her own way, slowly came to terms with the diagnosis, and began informing those close to her, including friends like Anil Dharker. 'She started telling me about how they had tried to brighten up a room with wallpaper at the Tata Memorial Hospital in Bombay,' Anil says. 'And I asked, well, why did you go there? And she replied, "Anil, don't you see? I've got the Big C." That was it. That was how I came to know.'

After her diagnosis, Jennifer had surgery in India and seemed to be recovering. But later, during a trip to London and after more check-ups, it appeared that the cancer had spread. Jennifer spent her last months in the British capital in the hospital and at her parents' home.

Geoffrey was devastated when she died. Jennifer was his firstborn, his favourite, his almost-all. A grieving Geoffrey mentions: 'The appalling loss is something I cannot talk or write about. It seemed as if the whole Land of Promise had frozen.'[5] Along with him, his wife, Laura Liddell Kendal, suffered. Felicity Kendal says, 'My mother was never quite the same afterwards. She was very religious before, but lost her faith. The light went out a bit.' The family, as a whole, found itself teetering, without a mainstay. 'My parents used to spend half the year in India with my sister,' Felicity states, 'but when she died, they felt going back was too painful, so they lost their home as well as Jennifer.'[6]

Felicity, in the meanwhile—who says, 'towards the end, Jennifer's only concern was for her children'—recalls being overwhelmed with grief; in a newspaper interview, she says of her sister: 'Our closeness came because we were nomads growing up, so didn't really have local friends. When [Jennifer] died, it wasn't just the tragedy of her death, it was also that selfish thing of, "Who am I going to say this to?" I couldn't make any decisions.'[7]

And then, there was Shashi. After Jennifer's demise, Dev Benegal says that he met Kunal Kapoor at a memorial at Prithvi Theatre: 'The family had just come back from Goa and Kunal said to me, "Dad took this boat out in the middle of the sea. When he got there, that was the first time he cried. Really, he wept."' Like Dev, I'm stunned by the rawness of that moment—of Shashi, alone in the vast open seas, sorrowing. 'He was really shaken by her death.'

Condolences poured in and there were press reports about Jennifer, the fine actress and grand woman. 'But few had seen what we had seen or had our memories,' Geoffrey writes. 'People's memories are over such a short period, and no one seems to imagine that anything really happens before their own time.'[8]

*

Shashi Kapoor continued to work after Jennifer Kendal Kapoor's passing, and some of his best work emerged during a time of loss. But something inside him did break. 'I think the death of Jennifer was a big blow to him,' Hanif Kureishi says, who worked with Shashi on *Sammy and Rosie Get Laid*[9] two years after his wife's demise. 'It really destroyed him.'

Jennifer had been the love of Shashi's life, his true anchor. With her death, he became rudderless. Simi Garewal tells me, 'Jennifer occupied—or Shashi surrendered to her—a large part of his personality. And they merged. With Jennifer gone, Shashi struggled, but couldn't find himself. That vast area of his personality that was Jennifer—now it lay empty. A void. I met him in London over dinner with Ismail Merchant and could see that he was floundering. He was different—not himself.'

Anil Dharker, always a friend, bore witness to Shashi's emotional collapse. Sometimes, the actor would depend on him—the way he must have, once, on Jennifer—to help him muddle through awkward social situations—such as, when the Ministry of Information and Broadcasting would request him to invite a foreign dignitary to dinner. 'And then he would ring me up,' Anil says, 'and implore: "Look, I have this very boring dinner guest, do you mind keeping me company?" And I would do that. But when the dignitary would leave, Shashi would actually push me out.'

Then, Anil, and those close to Shashi, bore witness to the actor's physical breakdown. Without the strict discipline Jennifer imposed on his existence, the star began indulging in his two chief weaknesses—food and drink. Anil remembers dropping by for lunch on occasion, and asking for a glass of beer, only to learn that Shashi had been drinking vodka since the morning. 'His domestic staff would bring refills as soon as his glass emptied out,' Anil says. 'He wouldn't even have to ask. They knew exactly how long it took him to finish his drink and they would be ready with the next. By the end of lunch, he would be quite sozzled.'

'I tried, quite often, to talk him out of it,' Anil continues. 'In fact, Sanjna and Kunal would say, "Come on, do something, he listens to you!" And I would respond, "This is one area where he *doesn't* listen to me at all." Then, they would say, "Visit more often because when you are here, at least he walks around. Otherwise, he just sits." So I did.'

As Shashi found himself caught in a loop of grief and consumption, he fell victim to that infamous Kapoor syndrome—of putting on too much weight, too soon. His health rapidly

deteriorated. He was forced to leave Atlas Apartments and moved
to Juhu, where he could be looked after by his son, Kunal. 'With
that, his whole life changed,' Madhu Jain tells me. 'He was a
South Bombay person,' and the move, she claims, added to the
star's loneliness, his growing depression. 'I went to Juhu a few
times,' Anil adds, 'but really, he stopped saying very much.' Simi,
with characteristic insight, tells me, 'It's as though Shashi had
given up the inner struggle. He almost became a recluse.'

Then came the year 2005. Ismail Merchant was dead; he was
only sixty-eight. 'Ismail was just one of those characters who was
supposed to live forever,' Sanjna says of the man who had become
part of her family. 'He was not meant to die. It was just wrong. I
am glad that I was physically with my dad when he heard the news.'

Shashi, when he found out about his beloved producer's demise,
was shaken; his grief became even more profound, loss piling on
loss. When James Ivory came to India a year later, paid his respects
at Ismail's grave, and then visited Shashi—the first leading man of
the Merchant–Ivory banner—he saw he was no longer the star he

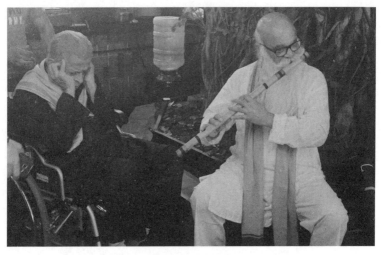

Shashi Kapoor immersed in music at Prithvi. Courtesy: Zoran Saher.

had known, but a ghost of a former self, emotionally withdrawn. 'I can't tell if it was a form of ongoing grieving about Jennifer,' James says. 'But Shashi's youth had dimmed, he was beginning to be an old man. We just didn't connect.'

Later, Simi saw Shashi at an award function at the Yash Raj Films Studios—the star, wheelchair-bound, his daughter by his side. As Simi approached her one-time co-star, Sanjna Kapoor cautioned her. 'She said to me, "He's had a stroke, so one side is paralyzed. He has also had a heart attack and lots of other problems. He doesn't remember people. So don't be upset. I'm just warning you."' Simi recalls.

Then she adds, 'To me, it didn't matter if Shashi remembered me, or if he didn't. I still had to go to him. I bent low, looked into his tired face. His eyes lifted slowly and focussed on me. He said, "Hello, Simi!" I felt like laughing…and crying. Then, I just wanted to hug him.'

As Simi speaks, it's as though I can hear echoes from Shashi's penultimate film,[10] the poetry of Hafeez Jalandhari:

Tarab-fizaa, alam-rubaa, asar sadaa-e-saaz kaa,
Jigar mein aag de lagaa.
Har ik lab pe ho sadaa, na haath rok saaqiyaa;
Pilaaye jaa, pilaaye jaa, pilaaye jaa—
Abhi to main jawaan hoon.

(Maker of song, sing through the night,
Kindle that fire in my life.
Maker of wine, ah, don't take flight;
Pour on, pour on, pour on—
For I'm still young tonight.)

Notes

1. Quoted in Surender Bhatia, 'Jennifer Kapoor is Back from Our Archives to Talk About Being in the Kapoor Khandaan', *Society*, 7 June 2013.
2. 1981, *36 Chowringhee Lane*, dir. Aparna Sen, prod. Shashi Kapoor, starring Jennifer Kendal, Debashree Roy, Dhritiman Chatterjee.
3. 1983, *Heat and Dust*, dir. James Ivory, prod. Ismail Merchant, starring Julie Christie, Greta Scacchi, Shashi Kapoor.
4. Geoffrey Kendal, *The Shakespeare Wallah: An Autobiography* (London: Sidgwich & Jackson, 1986), p. 172.
5. *Ibid.*
6. Quoted in Rebecca Hardy, 'How My Darling Sister's Death Changed My Life: Felicity Kendal Reveals How a Return Trip to India Stirred Up Childhood Memories', *Mail Online*, in <http://www.dailymail.co.uk/femail/article-2142393/Felicity-Kendal-reveals-return-trip-India-stirred-childhood-memories.html#ixzz3wwIvYyuZ>, accessed on 11 January 2016.
7. *Ibid.*
8. Geoffrey Kendal, *The Shakespeare Wallah: An Autobiography* (London: Sidgwich & Jackson, 1986), p. 173.
9. 1987, *Sammy and Rosie Get Laid*, dir. Stephen Frears, prod. Tim Bevan, Sarah Radclyffe, starring Shashi Kapoor, Frances Barber, Claire Bloom.
10. 1998, *Side Streets*, dir. Tony Gerber, prod. Bruce Weiss, starring Valeria Golino, Shashi Kapoor, Shabana Azmi.

THE SHASHI KAPOOR FILM LIST

A List of Films Starring Shashi Kapoor
Mentioned in this Book

1951, *Awara*, dir. Raj Kapoor, prod. Raj Kapoor, starring Prithviraj Kapoor, Raj Kapoor, Nargis, Shashi Kapoor.

1961, *Char Diwari*, dir. Krishan Chopra, prod. Jagan Prasad Sharma, starring Shashi Kapoor, Nanda, Manmohan Krishna.

1961, *Dharmputra*, dir. Yash Chopra, prod. B.R. Chopra, starring Shashi Kapoor, Mala Sinha, Rehman.

1962, *Prem Patra*, dir. Bimal Roy, prod. Bimal Roy, starring Shashi Kapoor, Sadhana, Seema Deo.

1963, *The Householder*, dir. James Ivory, prod. Ismail Merchant, starring Shashi Kapoor, Leela Naidu, Durga Khote.

1964, *Benazir*, dir. S. Khalil, prod. Bimal Roy, starring Ashok Kumar, Meena Kumari, Shashi Kapoor.

1965, *Jab Jab Phool Khile*, dir. Suraj Prakash, prod. Chetan K., starring Shashi Kapoor, Nanda, Agha.

1965, *Mohabbat Isko Kahete Hain*, dir. Akhtar Mirza, starring Nanda, Shashi Kapoor, Ramesh Deo.

1965, *Shakespeare Wallah*, dir. James Ivory, prod. Ismail Merchant, starring Shashi Kapoor, Felicity Kendal, Madhur Jaffrey.

1965, *Waqt*, dir. Yash Chopra, prod. B.R. Chopra, starring Balraj Sahni, Sharmila Tagore, Shashi Kapoor.

1966, *Pyar Kiye Jaa*, dir. C.V. Sridhar, starring Shashi Kapoor, Kalpana, Mumtaz.

1967, *Aamne Saamne*, dir. Suraj Prakash, prod. Suraj Prakash, starring Shashi Kapoor, Sharmila Tagore, Prem Chopra.

1967, *Pretty Polly*, dir. Guy Green, prod. George W. George, Frank Granat, starring Hayley Mills, Shashi Kapoor, Trevor Howard.

1968, *Haseena Maan Jayegi*, dir. Prakash Mehra, prod. S.M. Abbas, starring Shashi Kapoor, Babita, Johnny Walker.

1969, *Pyar Ka Mausam*, dir. Nasir Hussain, prod. Nasir Hussain, starring Shashi Kapoor, Asha Parekh, Bharat Bhushan.

1970, *Bombay Talkie*, dir. James Ivory, prod. Ismail Merchant, starring Shashi Kapoor, Jennifer Kendal, Zia Mohyeddin.

1970, *Suhana Safar*, dir. Vijay, prod. R.C. Kumar, starring Shashi Kapoor, Sharmila Tagore, Lalita Pawar.

1971, *Sharmeelee*, dir. Samir Ganguly, prod. Subodh Mukherji, starring Shashi Kapoor, Raakhee, Nazir Hussain.

1972, *Siddhartha*, dir. Conrad Rooks, prod. Conrad Rooks, starring Shashi Kapoor, Simi Garewal, Romesh Sharma.

1973, *Aa Gale Lag Jaa*, dir. Manmohan Desai, prod. A.K. Nadiadwala, starring Shashi Kapoor, Sharmila Tagore, Shatrughan Sinha.

1974, *Chor Machaye Shor*, dir. Ashok Roy, prod. N.N. Sippy, starring Shashi Kapoor, Mumtaz, Danny Denzongpa.

1974, *Paap Aur Punya*, dir. Prayag Raj, prod. Shyam Kumar Shivdasani, starring Shashi Kapoor, Sharmila Tagore, Aruna Irani.

1974, *Roti Kapada Aur Makaan*, dir. Manoj Kumar, prod. Manoj Kumar, starring Manoj Kumar, Shashi Kapoor, Amitabh Bachchan, Zeenat Aman.

1974, *Witness*, dir. Raj Marbros, starring Shashi Kapoor, Raakhee, Utpal Dutt.

1975, *Deewaar*, dir. Yash Chopra, prod. Gulshan Rai, starring Amitabh Bachchan, Shashi Kapoor, Neetu Singh, Parveen Babi.

1976, *Fakira*, dir. C.P. Dixit, prod. N.N. Sippy, starring Shashi Kapoor, Shabana Azmi, Danny Denzongpa.

1976, *Kabhi Kabhie*, dir. Yash Chopra, prod. Yash Chopra, starring Amitabh Bachchan, Shashi Kapoor, Raakhee, Simi Garewal, Waheeda Rehman, Rishi Kapoor, Neetu Singh.

1977, *Doosra Aadmi*, dir. Ramesh Talwar, prod. Yash Chopra, starring Rishi Kapoor, Raakhee, Shashi Kapoor, Neetu Singh.

1977, *Immaan Dharam*, dir. Desh Mukherjee, prod. Premji, starring Amitabh Bachchan, Shashi Kapoor, Sanjeev Kumar, Rekha.

1978, *Junoon*, dir. Shyam Benegal, prod. Shashi Kapoor, starring Shashi Kapoor, Shabana Azmi, Jennifer Kendal.

1978, *Satyam Shivam Sundaram*, dir. Raj Kapoor, prod. Raj Kapoor, starring Shashi Kapoor, Zeenat Aman, Padmini Kolhapure.

1978, *Trishul*, dir. Yash Chopra, prod. Gulshan Rai, starring Amitabh Bachchan, Shashi Kapoor, Hema Malini, Raakhee.

1979, *Gautam Govinda*, dir. Subhash Ghai, prod. Shyam Sunder Shivdasani, starring Shashi Kapoor, Shatrughan Sinha, Moushumi Chatterjee.

1979, *Kaala Patthar*, dir. Yash Chopra, prod. Yash Chopra, starring Amitabh Bachchan, Shashi Kapoor, Shatrughan Sinha, Neetu Singh, Parveen Babi.

1979, *Suhaag*, dir. Manmohan Desai, prod. Rajinder Kumar Sharma, Shakti Subhash Sharma, Prakash Trehan, starring Amitabh Bachchan, Shashi Kapoor, Rekha, Parveen Babi.

1980, *Shaan*, dir. Ramesh Sippy, prod. G.P. Sippy, starring Sunil Dutt, Amitabh Bachchan, Shashi Kapoor, Raakhee, Parveen Babi.

1981, *Kalyug*, dir. Shyam Benegal, prod. Shashi Kapoor, starring Shashi Kapoor, Rekha, Raj Babbar.

1981, *Silsila*, dir. Yash Chopra, prod. Yash Chopra, starring Amitabh Bachchan, Shashi Kapoor, Sanjeev Kumar, Rekha, Jaya Bhaduri.

1982, *Namak Halaal*, dir. Prakash Mehra, prod. Satyendra Pal, starring Amitabh Bachchan, Shashi Kapoor, Smita Patil, Waheeda Rehman, Parveen Babi.

1982, *Vijeta*, dir. Govind Nihalani, prod. Shashi Kapoor, starring Shashi Kapoor, Rekha, Kunal Kapoor.

1983, *Heat and Dust*, dir. James Ivory, prod. Ismail Merchant, starring Julie Christie, Greta Scacchi, Shashi Kapoor.

1986, *New Delhi Times*, dir. Ramesh Sharma, prod. P.K. Tiwari, starring Shashi Kapoor, Sharmila Tagore, Om Puri.

1987, *Sammy and Rosie Get Laid*, dir. Stephen Frears, prod. Tim Bevan, Sarah Radclyffe, starring Shashi Kapoor, Frances Barber, Claire Bloom.

1988, *The Deceivers*, dir. Nicholas Meyer, prod. Ismail Merchant, starring Pierce Brosnan, Shashi Kapoor, Saeed Jaffrey.

1993, *In Custody*, dir. Ismail Merchant, prod. Wahid Chowhan, starring Shashi Kapoor, Shabana Azmi, Om Puri.

1998, *Jinnah*, dir. Jamil Dehlavi, prod. Jamil Dehlavi, starring Christopher Lee, Shashi Kapoor, Maria Aitken.

1998, *Side Streets*, dir. Tony Gerber, prod. Bruce Weiss, starring Valeria Golino, Shashi Kapoor, Shabana Azmi.

1999, *Dirty British Boys*, dir. Assad Raja, prod. Fraz Hussain, starring George Christopher, Shashi Kapoor, Assad Raja.

A List of Films Produced by Shashi Kapoor Mentioned in this Book

1978, *Junoon*, dir. Shyam Benegal, prod. Shashi Kapoor, starring Shashi Kapoor, Shabana Azmi, Jennifer Kendal.

1981, *36 Chowringhee Lane*, dir. Aparna Sen, prod. Shashi Kapoor, starring Jennifer Kendal, Debashree Roy, Dhritiman Chatterjee.

1981, *Kalyug*, dir. Shyam Benegal, prod. Shashi Kapoor, starring Shashi Kapoor, Rekha, Raj Babbar.

1982, *Vijeta*, dir. Govind Nihalani, prod. Shashi Kapoor, starring Shashi Kapoor, Rekha, Kunal Kapoor.

1984, *Utsav*, dir. Girish Karnad, prod. Shashi Kapoor, starring Shekhar Suman, Rekha, Shashi Kapoor.

1991, *Ajooba*, dir. Shashi Kapoor, prod. Shashi Kapoor, starring Amitabh Bachchan, Rishi Kapoor, Dimple Kapadia.

The Only Film Directed by Shashi Kapoor Mentioned in this Book

1991, *Ajooba*, dir. Shashi Kapoor, prod. Shashi Kapoor, starring Amitabh Bachchan, Rishi Kapoor, Dimple Kapadia.

A List of Films Starring Shashi Kapoor
with Select Co-stars

Amitabh Bachchan

1974, *Roti Kapada Aur Makaan*, dir. Manoj Kumar, prod. Manoj Kumar, starring Manoj Kumar, Shashi Kapoor, Amitabh Bachchan, Zeenat Aman.

1975, *Deewaar*, dir. Yash Chopra, prod. Gulshan Rai, starring Amitabh Bachchan, Shashi Kapoor, Neetu Singh, Parveen Babi.

1976, *Kabhi Kabhie*, dir. Yash Chopra, prod. Yash Chopra, starring Amitabh Bachchan, Shashi Kapoor, Raakhee, Simi Garewal, Waheeda Rehman, Rishi Kapoor, Neetu Singh.

1977, *Immaan Dharam*, dir. Desh Mukherjee, prod. Premji, starring Amitabh Bachchan, Shashi Kapoor, Sanjeev Kumar, Rekha.

1978, *Trishul*, dir. Yash Chopra, prod. Gulshan Rai, starring Amitabh Bachchan, Shashi Kapoor, Hema Malini, Raakhee.

1979, *Ahsaas*, dir. Surindara Suri, prod. G.P. Sippy, starring Shashi Kapoor, Simi Garewal, Amitabh Bachchan.

1979, *Kaala Patthar*, dir. Yash Chopra, prod. Yash Chopra, starring Amitabh Bachchan, Shashi Kapoor, Shatrughan Sinha, Neetu Singh, Parveen Babi.

1979, *Suhaag*, dir. Manmohan Desai, prod. Rajinder Kumar Sharma, Shakti Subhash Sharma, Prakash Trehan, starring Amitabh Bachchan, Shashi Kapoor, Rekha, Parveen Babi.

1980, *Do Aur Do Paanch*, dir. Rakesh Kumar, prod. C. Dhandayuthapani, starring Amitabh Bachchan, Shashi Kapoor, Hema Malini, Parveen Babi.

1980, *Shaan*, dir. Ramesh Sippy, prod. G.P. Sippy, starring Sunil Dutt, Amitabh Bachchan, Shashi Kapoor, Raakhee, Parveen Babi.

1981, *Silsila*, dir. Yash Chopra, prod. Yash Chopra, starring Amitabh Bachchan, Shashi Kapoor, Sanjeev Kumar, Rekha, Jaya Bhaduri.

1982, *Namak Halaal*, dir. Prakash Mehra, prod. Satyendra Pal, starring Amitabh Bachchan, Shashi Kapoor, Smita Patil, Waheeda Rehman, Parveen Babi.

1991, *Akayla*, dir. Ramesh Sippy, prod. Mohammad Riaz, Mushir Alam, starring Amitabh Bachchan, Amrita Singh, Shashi Kapoor.

Asha Parekh

1968, *Kanyadaan*, dir. Mohan Segal, prod. Rajendra Bhatia, starring Asha Parekh, Shashi Kapoor, Bela Bose.

1969, *Pyar Ka Mausam*, dir. Nasir Hussain, prod. Nasir Hussain, starring Shashi Kapoor, Asha Parekh, Bharat Bhushan.

Babita

1968, *Haseena Maan Jayegi*, dir. Prakash Mehra, prod. S.M. Abbas, starring Shashi Kapoor, Babita, Johnny Walker.

1969, *Ek Shriman Ek Shrimati*, dir. Bhappi Sonie, prod. Surinder Kapoor, starring Shashi Kapoor, Babita, Prem Chopra.

Hema Malini

1969, *Jahan Pyar Mile*, dir. Lekh Tandon, prod. Lekh Tandon, starring Shashi Kapoor, Hema Malini, Nadira.

1970, *Abhinetri*, dir. Subodh Mukherji, prod. Subodh Mukherji, starring Shashi Kapoor, Hema Malini, Deb Mukherjee.

1976, *Aap Beati*, dir. Mohan Kumar, prod. Mohan Kumar, starring Shashi Kapoor, Hema Malini, Ashok Kumar.

1976, *Naach Uthe Sansaar*, dir. Yakub Hasan Rizvi, prod. Mohmud Sarosh, starring Shashi Kapoor, Hema Malini, Simi Garewal.

1978, *Apna Khoon*, dir. Babbar Subhash, prod. S.K. Kapur, starring Shashi Kapoor, Hema Malini, Ashok Kumar.

1978, *Trishul*, dir. Yash Chopra, prod. Gulshan Rai, starring Amitabh Bachchan, Shashi Kapoor, Hema Malini, Raakhee.

1980, *Do Aur Do Paanch*, dir. Rakesh Kumar, prod. C. Dhandayuthapani, starring Amitabh Bachchan, Shashi Kapoor, Hema Malini, Parveen Babi.

1981, *Kranti*, dir. Manoj Kumar, prod. Manoj Kumar, starring Shashi Kapoor, Dilip Kumar, Hema Malini, Parveen Babi.

1981, *Krodhi*, dir. Subhash Ghai, prod. Ranjit Virk, starring Shashi Kapoor, Zeenat Aman, Hema Malini.

1981, *Maan Gaye Ustad*, dir. Shibu Mitra, prod. S.K. Kapur, starring Shashi Kapoor, Hema Malini, Amjad Khan.

1985, *Aandhi-Toofan*, dir. Babbar Subhash, prod. Pahlaj Nihalani, starring Shashi Kapoor, Hema Malini, Danny Denzongpa.

1987, *Anjaam*, dir. T. Hariharan, prod. Ramesh Tiwari, starring Shashi Kapoor, Hema Malini, Satish Shah.

Meena Kumari

1964, *Benazir*, dir. S. Khalil, prod. Bimal Roy, starring Ashok Kumar, Meena Kumari, Shashi Kapoor.

Mumtaz

1974, *Chor Machaye Shor*, dir. Ashok Roy, prod. N.N. Sippy, starring Shashi Kapoor, Mumtaz, Danny Denzongpa.

1975, *Prem Kahani*, dir. Raj Khosla, prod. Lekhraj Khosla, starring Rajesh Khanna, Shashi Kapoor, Mumtaz.

Nanda

1961, *Char Diwari*, dir. Krishan Chopra, prod. Jagan Prasad Sharma, starring Shashi Kapoor, Nanda, Manmohan Krishna.

1962, *Mehndi Lagi Mere Haath*, dir. Suraj Prakash, prod. Hiren Khera, starring Ashok Kumar, Nanda, Shashi Kapoor.

1965, *Jab Jab Phool Khile*, dir. Suraj Prakash, prod. Chetan K., starring Shashi Kapoor, Nanda, Agha.

1965, *Mohabbat Isko Kahete Hain*, dir. Akhtar Mirza, starring Nanda, Shashi Kapoor, Ramesh Deo.

1966, *Neend Hamari Khwab Tumhare*, dir. Shiv Sahni, prod. Hans Choudhary, starring Shashi Kapoor, Nanda, Balraj Sahni.

1968, *Juari*, dir. Suraj Prakash, prod. Nirmal Sirkar, starring Shashi Kapoor, Nanda, Tanuja.

1969, *Raja Saab*, dir. Suraj Prakash, prod. Limelight, starring Shashi Kapoor, Nanda, Kamal Kapoor.

1970, *Rootha Na Karo*, dir. Sunder Dar, prod. Bishwanath Prasad Shahabadi, starring Shashi Kapoor, Nanda, Kumari Naaz.

Neetu Singh

1975, *Deewaar*, dir. Yash Chopra, prod. Gulshan Rai, starring Amitabh Bachchan, Shashi Kapoor, Neetu Singh, Parveen Babi.

1976, *Kabhi Kabhie*, dir. Yash Chopra, prod. Yash Chopra, starring Amitabh Bachchan, Shashi Kapoor, Raakhee, Simi Garewal, Waheeda Rehman, Rishi Kapoor, Neetu Singh.

1976, *Shankar Dada*, dir. Shibu Mitra, prod. S.K. Kapur, starring Shashi Kapoor, Neetu Singh, Ashok Kumar.

1977, *Doosra Aadmi*, dir. Ramesh Talwar, prod. Yash Chopra, starring Rishi Kapoor, Raakhee, Shashi Kapoor, Neetu Singh.

1978, *Heeralal Pannalal*, dir. Ashok Roy, prod. Ashok Roy, starring Shashi Kapoor, Zeenat Aman, Neetu Singh.

1979, *Duniya Meri Jeb Mein*, dir. Tinnu Anand, prod. Bitu Anand, Naresh Malhotra, starring Rishi Kapoor, Shashi Kapoor, Neetu Singh.

1979, *Kaala Patthar*, dir. Yash Chopra, prod. Yash Chopra, starring Amitabh Bachchan, Shashi Kapoor, Shatrughan Sinha, Neetu Singh, Parveen Babi.

1980, *Kala Pani*, dir. Shibu Mitra, prod. B. Gupta, starring Shashi Kapoor, Neetu Singh, Ajit.

1981, *Ek Aur Ek Gyarah*, dir. Ashok Roy, starring Shashi Kapoor, Neetu Singh, Vinod Khanna.

1982, *Do Guru*, dir. Ravi Tandon, starring Shashi Kapoor, Neetu Singh, Pran.

Parveen Babi

1975, *Deewaar*, dir. Yash Chopra, prod. Gulshan Rai, starring Amitabh Bachchan, Shashi Kapoor, Neetu Singh, Parveen Babi.

1978, *Aahuti*, dir. Ashok V. Bhushan, prod. Ramchand Bashomal, Reeta Shah, R. Soni, starring Rajendra Kumar, Shashi Kapoor, Parveen Babi.

1979, *Chor Sipahee*, dir. Prayag Raj, prod. Shyam Sunder Shivdasani, starring Shashi Kapoor, Parveen Babi, Shabana Azmi.

1979, *Kaala Patthar*, dir. Yash Chopra, prod. Yash Chopra, starring Amitabh Bachchan, Shashi Kapoor, Shatrughan Sinha, Neetu Singh, Parveen Babi.

1979, *Suhaag*, dir. Manmohan Desai, prod. Rajinder Kumar Sharma, Shakti Subhash Sharma, Prakash Trehan, starring Amitabh Bachchan, Shashi Kapoor, Rekha, Parveen Babi.

1980, *Do Aur Do Paanch*, dir. Rakesh Kumar, prod. C. Dhandayuthapani, starring Amitabh Bachchan, Shashi Kapoor, Hema Malini, Parveen Babi.

1980, *Shaan*, dir. Ramesh Sippy, prod. G.P. Sippy, starring Sunil Dutt, Amitabh Bachchan, Shashi Kapoor, Raakhee, Parveen Babi.

1981, *Kranti*, dir. Manoj Kumar, prod. Manoj Kumar, starring Shashi Kapoor, Dilip Kumar, Hema Malini, Parveen Babi.

1982, *Namak Halaal*, dir. Prakash Mehra, prod. Satyendra Pal, starring Amitabh Bachchan, Shashi Kapoor, Smita Patil, Waheeda Rehman, Parveen Babi.

1983, *Durdesh*, dir. Ambrish Sangal, prod. Shamim Ahmed, Jagdish Bharoos, starring Shashi Kapoor, Sharmila Tagore, Parveen Babi.

Raakhee

1971, *Sharmeelee*, dir. Samir Ganguly, prod. Subodh Mukherji, starring Shashi Kapoor, Raakhee, Nazir Hussain.

1972, *Jaanwar Aur Insaan*, dir. Tapi Chanakya, prod. Sandow M.M.A. Chinnappa Devar, starring Shashi Kapoor, Raakhee, Shabnam.

1974, *Witness*, dir. Raj Marbros, starring Shashi Kapoor, Raakhee, Utpal Dutt.

1976, *Kabhi Kabhie*, dir. Yash Chopra, starring Amitabh Bachchan, Shashi Kapoor, Raakhee, Simi Garewal, Waheeda Rehman, Rishi Kapoor, Neetu Singh.

1977, *Doosra Aadmi*, dir. Ramesh Talwar, prod. Yash Chopra, starring Rishi Kapoor, Raakhee, Shashi Kapoor, Neetu Singh.

1978, *Trishna*, dir. Anil Ganguli, prod. G.P. Sippy, starring Shashi Kapoor, Sanjeev Kumar, Raakhee.

1978, *Trishul*, dir. Yash Chopra, prod. Gulshan Rai, starring Amitabh Bachchan, Shashi Kapoor, Hema Malini, Raakhee.

1980, *Shaan*, dir. Ramesh Sippy, prod. G.P. Sippy, starring Sunil Dutt, Amitabh Bachchan, Shashi Kapoor, Raakhee, Parveen Babi.

1981, *Baseraa*, dir. Ramesh Talwar, prod. Ramesh Behl, starring Shashi Kapoor, Raakhee, Rekha.

1983, *Bandhan Kuchchey Dhaagon Ka,* dir. Anil Sharma, prod. K.C. Sharma, starring Shashi Kapoor, Raakhee, Zeenat Aman.

1984, *Bandh Honth,* dir. Raj Marbros, starring Utpal Dutt, Shashi Kapoor, Raakhee.

1984, *Zameen Aasmaan,* dir. Bharat Rangachary, prod. Subhash Gupta, Uday Narayan Singh, starring Shashi Kapoor, Raakhee, Rekha.

1985, *Pighalta Aasman,* dir. Shammi, prod. Shammi, starring Shashi Kapoor, Raakhee, Rati Agnihotri.

Rekha

1977, *Chakkar Pe Chakkar,* dir. Ashok Roy, prod. S. Jagdish Chandra, starring Shashi Kapoor, Rekha, Pran.

1977, *Farishta Aur Qatil,* dir. S.M. Abbas, prod. Ziaul Hasan, Mohd. Ilyas, starring Shashi Kapoor, Rekha, Bindu.

1977, *Immaan Dharam,* dir. Desh Mukherjee, prod. Premji, starring Amitabh Bachchan, Shashi Kapoor, Sanjeev Kumar, Rekha.

1978, *Do Musafir,* dir. Devendra Goel, prod. Syed Anwar Hussain, R.N. Kumar, Shashikant Shah, starring Shashi Kapoor, Rekha, Ashok Kumar.

1978, *Muqaddar,* dir. Ravi Tandon, starring Shashi Kapoor, Rekha, Amjad Khan.

1978, *Rahu Ketu,* dir. B.R. Ishara, prod. B.D. Pandey, starring Shashi Kapoor, Rekha, Bindu.

1979, *Suhaag,* dir. Manmohan Desai, prod. Rajinder Kumar Sharma, Shakti Subhash Sharma, Prakash Trehan, starring Amitabh Bachchan, Shashi Kapoor, Rekha, Parveen Babi.

1980, *Kali Ghata,* dir. Ved Rahi, prod. Ved Rahi, starring Shashi Kapoor, Rekha, Danny Denzongpa.

1980, *Neeyat*, dir. Anil Ganguly, prod. Veer Jain, Tutu Sharma, starring Shashi Kapoor, Rekha, Jeetendra.

1981, *Baseraa*, dir. Ramesh Talwar, prod. Ramesh Behl, starring Shashi Kapoor, Raakhee, Rekha.

1981, *Kalyug*, dir. Shyam Benegal, prod. Shashi Kapoor, starring Shashi Kapoor, Rekha, Raj Babbar.

1981, *Silsila*, dir. Yash Chopra, prod. Yash Chopra, starring Amitabh Bachchan, Shashi Kapoor, Sanjeev Kumar, Rekha, Jaya Bhaduri.

1982, *Vijeta*, dir. Govind Nihalani, prod. Shashi Kapoor, starring Shashi Kapoor, Rekha, Kunal Kapoor.

1984, *Utsav*, dir. Girish Karnad, prod. Shashi Kapoor, starring Shekhar Suman, Rekha, Shashi Kapoor.

1984, *Zameen Aasmaan*, dir. Bharat Rangachary, prod. Subhash Gupta, Uday Narayan Singh, starring Shashi Kapoor, Raakhee, Rekha.

1987, *Ijaazat*, dir. Gulzar, prod. R.K. Gupta, starring Rekha, Naseeruddin Shah, Shashi Kapoor.

1987, *Pyar Ki Jeet*, dir. Saawan Kumar Tak, prod. Saawan Kumar Tak, starring Shashi Kapoor, Rekha, Vinod Mehra.

1989, *Clerk*, dir. Manoj Kumar, prod. Manoj Kumar, starring Manoj Kumar, Rekha, Shashi Kapoor.

Rishi Kapoor

1976, *Kabhi Kabhie*, dir. Yash Chopra, prod. Yash Chopra, starring Amitabh Bachchan, Shashi Kapoor, Raakhee, Simi Garewal, Waheeda Rehman, Rishi Kapoor, Neetu Singh.

1977, *Doosra Aadmi*, dir. Ramesh Talwar, prod. Yash Chopra, starring Rishi Kapoor, Raakhee, Shashi Kapoor, Neetu Singh.

1979, *Duniya Meri Jeb Mein*, dir. Tinnu Anand, prod. Bitu Anand, Naresh Malhotra, starring Rishi Kapoor, Shashi Kapoor, Neetu Singh.

Sadhana

1962, *Prem Patra*, dir. Bimal Roy, prod. Bimal Roy, starring Shashi Kapoor, Sadhana, Seema Deo.

Shabana Azmi

1976, *Fakira*, dir. C.P. Dixit, prod. N.N. Sippy, starring Shashi Kapoor, Shabana Azmi, Danny Denzongpa.

1977, *Hira Aur Patthar*, dir. Vijay Bhatt, prod. Arun Bhatt, Kishore Vyas, starring Ashok Kumar, Shashi Kapoor, Shabana Azmi.

1978, *Atithee*, dir. Aravind Sen, prod. Anita Sen, Aravind Sen, starring Shashi Kapoor, Shabana Azmi, Shatrughan Sinha.

1978, *Junoon*, dir. Shyam Benegal, prod. Shashi Kapoor, starring Shashi Kapoor, Shabana Azmi, Jennifer Kendal.

1979, *Chor Sipahee*, dir. Prayag Raj, prod. Shyam Sunder Shivdasani, starring Shashi Kapoor, Parveen Babi, Shabana Azmi.

1989, *Oonch Neech*, dir. Wasi Khan, prod. Jagdish Varma, starring Shashi Kapoor, Shabana Azmi, Sanjeev Kumar.

1993, *In Custody*, dir. Ismail Merchant, prod. Wahid Chowhan, starring Shashi Kapoor, Shabana Azmi, Om Puri.

1998, *Side Streets*, dir. Tony Gerber, prod. Bruce Weiss, starring Valeria Golino, Shashi Kapoor, Shabana Azmi.

Sharmila Tagore

1965, *Waqt*, dir. Yash Chopra, prod. B.R. Chopra, starring Balraj Sahni, Sharmila Tagore, Shashi Kapoor.

1967, *Aamne Saamne*, dir. Suraj Prakash, prod. Suraj Prakash, starring Shashi Kapoor, Sharmila Tagore, Prem Chopra.

1970, *My Love*, dir. S. Sukhdev, starring Shashi Kapoor, Sharmila Tagore, Rajendra Nath.

1970, *Suhana Safar*, dir. Vijay, prod. R.C. Kumar, starring Shashi Kapoor, Sharmila Tagore, Lalita Pawar.

1973, *Aa Gale Lag Jaa*, dir. Manmohan Desai, prod. A.K. Nadiadwala, starring Shashi Kapoor, Sharmila Tagore, Shatrughan Sinha.

1974, *Paap Aur Punya*, dir. Prayag Raj, prod. Shyam Kumar Shivdasani, starring Shashi Kapoor, Sharmila Tagore, Aruna Irani.

1975, *Anari*, dir. Asit Sen, prod. Satish Bhatia, Inder Kapoor, starring Shashi Kapoor, Sharmila Tagore, Kabir Bedi.

1983, *Durdesh*, dir. Ambrish Sangal, prod. Shamim Ahmed, Jagdish Bharoos, starring Shashi Kapoor, Sharmila Tagore, Parveen Babi.

1986, *New Delhi Times*, dir. Ramesh Sharma, prod. P.K. Tiwari, starring Shashi Kapoor, Sharmila Tagore, Om Puri.

1986, *Swati*, dir. Kranthi Kumar, prod. L.V. Prasad, starring Shashi Kapoor, Sharmila Tagore, Meenakshi Sheshadri.

Simi Garewal

1972, *Siddhartha*, dir. Conrad Rooks, prod. Conrad Rooks, starring Shashi Kapoor, Simi Garewal, Romesh Sharma.

1976, *Kabhi Kabhie*, dir. Yash Chopra, prod. Yash Chopra, starring Amitabh Bachchan, Shashi Kapoor, Raakhee, Simi Garewal, Waheeda Rehman, Rishi Kapoor, Neetu Singh.

1979, *Ahsaas*, dir. Surindara Suri, prod. G.P. Sippy, starring Shashi Kapoor, Simi Garewal, Amitabh Bachchan.

Waheeda Rehman

1976, *Kabhi Kabhie*, dir. Yash Chopra, prod. Yash Chopra, starring Amitabh Bachchan, Shashi Kapoor, Raakhee, Simi Garewal, Waheeda Rehman, Rishi Kapoor, Neetu Singh.

1982, *Namak Halaal*, dir. Prakash Mehra, prod. Satyendra Pal, starring Amitabh Bachchan, Shashi Kapoor, Smita Patil, Waheeda Rehman, Parveen Babi.

1982, *Sawaal*, dir. Ramesh Talwar, prod. Yash Chopra, starring Shashi Kapoor, Sanjeev Kumar, Waheeda Rehman.

Zeenat Aman

1974, *Roti Kapada Aur Makaan*, dir. Manoj Kumar, prod. Manoj Kumar, starring Manoj Kumar, Shashi Kapoor, Amitabh Bachchan, Zeenat Aman.

1976, *Deewaangee*, dir. Samir Ganguly, prod. Subodh Mukherji, starring Shashi Kapoor, Zeenat Aman, Helen.

1978, *Heeralal Pannalal*, dir. Ashok Roy, prod. Ashok Roy, starring Shashi Kapoor, Zeenat Aman, Neetu Singh.

1978, *Satyam Shivam Sundaram*, dir. Raj Kapoor, prod. Raj Kapoor, starring Shashi Kapoor, Zeenat Aman, Padmini Kolhapure.

1981, *Krodhi*, dir. Subhash Ghai, prod. Ranjit Virk, starring Shashi Kapoor, Zeenat Aman, Hema Malini.

1983, *Bandhan Kuchchey Dhaagon Ka*, dir. Anil Sharma, prod. K.C. Sharma, starring Shashi Kapoor, Zeenat Aman, Raakhee.

1984, *Pakhandi*, dir. Samir Ganguly, prod. Robert D'Souza, starring Shashi Kapoor, Sanjeev Kumar, Zeenat Aman.

1985, *Bhavani Junction*, dir. H. Dinesh, prod. Deepak S. Shivdasani, starring Shashi Kapoor, Shatrughan Sinha, Zeenat Aman.

1986, *Aurat*, dir. B.R. Ishara, prod. Sunil Bohra, starring Zeenat Aman, Shashi Kapoor, Shakti Kapoor.

Acknowledgements

While I did not approach Shashi Kapoor for an interview, many people who knew him and worked with him were more than happy to speak about the man, the actor, the star.

This book would not have been possible without the interviews I conducted with the following people: Feroz Abbas Khan, Shabana Azmi, Amitabh Bachchan, Dev Benegal, Shyam Benegal, Pamela Chopra, Jamil Dehlavi, Anil Dharker, Sabrina Dhawan, Rachel Dwyer, Stephen Frears, Simi Garewal, Rohena Gera, Tony Gerber, James (Jim) Ivory, Madhur Jaffrey, Madhu Jain, Kunal Kapoor, Neetu Singh Kapoor, Rishi Kapoor, Sanjna Kapoor, Sameera Khan, Hanif Kureishi, David McKibben, Govind Nihalani, Lynn Nottage, Alexander Rooks, Aparna Sen, Ramesh Sharma, Sharmila Tagore, Ramesh Talwar and Beth Watkins. I am grateful to each of them for sharing with me their memories and thoughts about Shashi Kapoor. I am especially thankful to Shabana Azmi and Madhu Jain who encouraged me by saying that a book in appreciation of Shashi was essential.

Special thanks to my editor, Dharini Bhaskar, who was excited about the project even as I shared images of a young Shashi Kapoor with her.

I am grateful to Karan Johar for his evocative foreword, and to Spandan Banerjee for designing a beautiful cover.

I am also grateful to the following people who advised me, sent me research material and DVDs while I was writing this book, shared contact information and even made interviews possible—

Dheeraj Akolkar, Parag and Bela Amladi, Peter Becker, Meenal Baghal, Girimohan Coneti, Zette Emmons, Zakir Hussain, Amit Khanna, Ronjita Kulkarni, Amitava Kumar, Nikhil Lakshman, Rajeev Masand, Tim McHenry, Amitava Nag, Pritish Nandy, Avtar Panesar, Ram Rahman, Vaibhav Rajput, Zoran Saher, Gingger Shankar, Aroon Shivdasani, Sree Sreenivasan and Suphala.

Some parts of the book were written and researched in the summer of 2015, when my mother was in a hospital in Noida and I had time to focus on my work. I must thank my cousins, Rakesh and Sonal Popli, for feeding me during those days and later over autumn, when I moved in next to their apartment.

I am thankful to my writer and actor-friend, Rupleena Bose, who suggested the title of this book to me. And my friend, Girimohan Coneti, who let me stay in his apartment in Brooklyn for weeks, while I sat up late watching many of Shashi's films.

I must thank Megha Bhouraskar for sharing her passion for Shashi Kapoor with me.

And finally, thanks to Dev Benegal for always keeping me abreast of stories in Bombay's film industry.